International Schooling

Also available from Bloomsbury

Critical Human Rights, Citizenship, and Democracy Education: Entanglements and Regenerations edited by Michalinos Zembylas and André Keet

Educating for Durable Solutions: Histories of Schooling in Kenya's Dadaab and Kakuma Refugee Camps by Christine Monoghan

Educating for Peace and Human Rights: An Introduction by Maria Hantzopoulos and Monisha Bajaj

Identities and Education: Comparative Perspectives in Times of Crisis edited by Stephen Carney and Eleftherios Klerides

Language and Decoloniality in Higher Education: Reclaiming Voices from the South edited by Zannie Bock and Christopher Stroud

Low-fee Private Schooling and Poverty in Developing Countries by Joanna Härmä

Non-University Higher Education: Geographies of Place, Possibility and Inequality by Holly Henderson

Schooling as Uncertainty: An Ethnographic Memoir in Comparative Education by Frances Vavrus

The Bloomsbury Handbook of Global Education and Learning edited by Douglas Bourn

The Bloomsbury Handbook of Theory in Comparative and International Education edited by Tavis D. Jules, Robin Shields and Matthew A. M. Thomas

The Bloomsbury Handbook of the Internationalization of Higher Education in the Global South edited by Juliet Thondhlana, Evelyn Chiyevo Garwe, Hans de Wit, Jocelyne Gacel-Ávila, Futao Huang and Wondwosen Tamrat

International Schooling

Privilege and Power in Globalized Societies

Lucy Bailey

BLOOMSBURY ACADEMIC
LONDON · NEW YORK · OXFORD · NEW DELHI · SYDNEY

BLOOMSBURY ACADEMIC
Bloomsbury Publishing Plc
50 Bedford Square, London, WC1B 3DP, UK
1385 Broadway, New York, NY 10018, USA
29 Earlsfort Terrace, Dublin 2, Ireland

BLOOMSBURY, BLOOMSBURY ACADEMIC and the Diana logo are
trademarks of Bloomsbury Publishing Plc

First published in Lucy Bailey, 2022
This paperback edition published in 2023

Copyright © Lucy Bailey, 2022

Lucy Bailey has asserted her right under the Copyright, Designs and
Patents Act, 1988, to be identified as Author of this work.

All rights reserved. No part of this publication may be reproduced or
transmitted in any form or by any means, electronic or mechanical, including
photocopying, recording, or any information storage or retrieval system,
without prior permission in writing from the publishers.

Bloomsbury Publishing Plc does not have any control over, or responsibility for,
any third-party websites referred to or in this book. All internet addresses given
in this book were correct at the time of going to press. The author and publisher
regret any inconvenience caused if addresses have changed or sites have
ceased to exist, but can accept no responsibility for any such changes.

A catalogue record for this book is available from the British Library.

Library of Congress Cataloging-in-Publication Data
Names: Bailey, Lucy E. author.
Title: International schooling: privilege and power in globalised
societies / Lucy Bailey.
Description: New York; London: Bloomsbury Academic, 2021. |
Includes bibliographical references and index.
Identifiers: LCCN 2021011676 (print) | LCCN 2021011677 (ebook) |
ISBN 9781350169999 (Hardback) | ISBN 9781350170001 (eBook) |
ISBN 9781350170018 (ePub)
Subjects: LCSH: International schools–Cross-cultural studies. |
Education and globalization.
Classification: LCC LC1090.B35 2021 (print) |
LCC LC1090 (ebook) | DDC 370.116–dc23
LC record available at https://lccn.loc.gov/2021011676
LC ebook record available at https://lccn.loc.gov/2021011677

ISBN: HB: 978-1-3501-6999-9
PB : 978-1-3502-2495-7
ePDF: 978-1-3501-7000-1
eBook: 978-1-3501-7001-8

Typeset by Integra Software Services Pvt. Ltd.

To find out more about our authors and books visit
www.bloomsbury.com and sign up for our newsletters.

To Simon, Analysia, Miranne, Katiyah and Pietta

Contents

Introduction		1
1	Globalization, Education and the International Schools Movement	7
2	Conceptualizing the International School	25
3	The Micropolitics of International Schools	41
4	Teaching in International Schools	61
5	Internationalism or Westernization?	77
6	Educating for Global Citizenship	93
7	Inequalities and International Schools	113
8	International Education and International Schools: New Theorizations	131
Conclusion		149
References		154
Index		174

Introduction

There has always been a fascination with the relationship between schooling and power. Indeed, the entrancement is a rare example of alignment between academic interest and the popular imagination. Whether it is images of schoolboys at Eton in their extraordinary tailcoats and starched collars, or stories of the Quaker traditions at Sidwell Friends (the school attended by the Obama girls, Chelsea Clinton, and the offspring of many other US Presidents), there is a strange voyeurism in seeing the preparation of a small child, or a young adult, for a life of privilege.

Although the preparation process has evolved, its success in securing privilege for the next generation has been remarkably successful for centuries, seemingly resistant to transformation in both the nature of society and in schooling itself. As Fordist mass production has given way to the post-Fordist knowledge economy, as both production and consumption have been globalized, as new social movements asserting previously marginalized identities have emerged, and as environmental movements have called for fundamental changes in capitalistic exchange, each year another cohort of schoolchildren has graduated from school largely to slot into the social positions occupied by their parents. And this has continued to happen despite an avowed intention in many societies to give every child a chance, to ensure meritocracy, to use schools as the guarantee of equality of opportunity.

Sociologists of education have sought to explain the persisting role of education in the reproduction of privilege (Bourdieu, 1998; Courtois, 2017). Until the 1970s, the focus was largely on the cognitive advantages given by high-quality elite education, as well as the networks that children could forge in these schools. To address this inequality, huge effort was placed into offering opportunities for academic excellence in government schools and reducing the influence of old-boy networks on access to work and university. In the UK, the introduction of comprehensive schools in the same period was intended to ensure that all children had access to the same kind of school. However, the persistence of inequalities despite these efforts led theorists from the 1970s onwards to focus attention on the more covert ways in which schools are implicated in the reproduction of privilege and power. The ideas of social capital, correspondence theory and the hidden curriculum are amongst those that appealed to sociologists of education in the 1970s and 1980s. These conceptual frameworks have influenced contemporary ways of understanding elite education (Brown & Lauder, 2011; Brooks & Waters, 2015; Khalil & Kelly, 2020), even as recent post-structuralist research has made more attention to accounts of how students actively construct their identities, acknowledging the importance of fluidity in narratives and acknowledging multiple ways in which elite students could be marginalized on the basis of ethnicity, sexuality and gender (e.g. Forbes & Weiner, 2014). These accounts have, in summary, sought to offer a more nuanced exploration of the relationship between elite education and power (Kenway & Koh, 2013).

The study of international schooling is, as I shall argue in this book, an integral and increasingly important part of this nuanced exploration. International schooling is rapidly increasing in importance as a form of elite education as the number of international schools increases, and the countries in which international schooling is expanding gain greater influence over the world economy; in many of these countries, international schooling has become integral to the education of the national elite. In addition, international schooling enables the mobility that is the bedrock of this global capitalism, so that it serves the globally mobile elite (Bates, 2011a). So study of international schooling focuses both on the education of national elites in some countries (Song, 2013; Bailey, 2018), and also on those who remain or have become privileged internationally as globalization transforms our world (Gardner-McTaggart, 2016). There are, as we shall see, many different types of international schools, some catering to diplomatic and corporate elites, others educating the upper-class and nobility, still others more widely accessible as they school the middle-class across large parts of Asia (Bailey, 2018). In some, the continuity with national elite schooling is made explicit as they are international off-shoots of an exclusive British public school (Bunnell, Courtois & Donnelly, 2020). Despite these diverse themes within international schooling, there are important commonalities that will feature in the analysis throughout this book; for instance, one commonality across diverse international schools is an emphasis on character formation, whereby the modes of conduct needed for elite society are instilled (Loh, 2016; Bunnell, 2020). Another example is the emphasis on the brand/name/image in international schooling; in a globalized world of education and employment, where employers cannot be expected to know every school or university, the branding of elite education becomes key (Brown et al., 2008).

For those who seek to understand the relationship between schooling and privilege in our globalized world, study of international schools matters (Bunnell, 2020). Put simply, the argument in this book is twofold. First, that international schools provide insights into the operation of global capitalism. They mirror current inequalities. They provide a microscope under which we can examine the operation of power. Second, that international schools are key sites in which access to global power is seized and legitimated, and thereby they shape the future of global capitalism – by educating children to find their place in the global elite (Lee & Wright, 2016), they help to choose the powerful and to shape the values of those who will hold power in the future. Throughout this work, we will discover ways in which international schools differ from the exclusive public schools which educated past elites; we will see that their ethos and stated missions, their teachers and leaders, their forms of curriculum and assessment all indicate a realignment of national identities and priorities in relation to global forces.

Mass systems of education in countries around the world developed to meet the social and economic needs of the emerging nation state (Green, 2013). International schooling has expanded rapidly to become another mass system of education with 6 million students worldwide now educated in international schools (ISC Research, 2020a). However, the social and economic factors driving the development of international schooling, the distinctive characteristics of international schools and the challenges faced by those engaged in the educational aspiration to be 'international' remain largely obscure. There is, nevertheless, a steadily growing literature focused on this issue, and this book contributes to the literature seeking to shine a light on these issues. With most of the students in these schools now being passport-holders from the country in which the school is located rather than a mobile, expatriate population (ISC Research, 2020b), it is unclear what is meant by being 'international', nor whether international schools with changing demographics find this a contested concept. Although international schooling had its origins in part in market demands from mobile executives and in part in ideological aspirations to promote internationalism and intercultural understanding, its form and function are arguably changing (Hayden & Thompson, 2008). The international school sector offers contradictory potential, being in part a progressive movement to promote internationalism and intercultural understanding – many involved in the international school sector have a commitment to social change – and in part a system through which structural inequalities are replicated, or even accentuated, by its role in the perpetuation of privilege and also the creation of a new global elite.

This book critically analyses the concept of international schooling and its exponential growth in the twenty-first century. It identifies the forces driving this trend, asking to what extent this is an enterprise that meets the needs of a global elite and examining its relationship to national systems of education. It asks to what extent these are distinct institutions by examining the experiences of key stakeholders. The book discusses how wider social inequalities around socio-economic difference, ethnicity, 'race' and gender are reproduced through international schooling. It examines the theory that 'international' curricula are in fact Western curricula and considers the impact of international schools on social and cultural inequalities. Having researched international schools across Asia, the Middle East, Europe, North and South America, and Africa, I explore ways in which international schools adapt to local cultural contexts and examine the views of parents, students, teachers and school leaders towards the education that they provide (Bailey, 2015a; Bailey & Cooker, 2019; Bailey & Gibson, 2019). This book identifies the ways in which the diverse educational institutions that claim to be international schools – and this includes state schools, private schools, elite international schools, and religious schools – conceptualize international schooling.

To do this, I draw on a range of 'examples' from research studies into international schools that I have conducted with my colleagues over the last ten years. Some of these studies were independent projects, whilst others were funded by the International Baccalaureate Organisation. The research methodologies employed in each study varied but are available for scrutiny in the IB reports published online and in the peer-reviewed articles my colleagues and I have published in international journals. Over the course of these projects, I personally have interviewed hundreds of international school teachers, students, parents and leaders; I have conducted focus groups with these stakeholders; I have developed surveys collecting data from hundreds of more teachers, students and parents. I have personally collected data during school visits to international schools in Malaysia, Bahrain, Singapore, Thailand, China, Indonesia and the UAE. My colleagues have conducted research visits to additional countries, including the UK, the United States, Mexico, Kenya, Spain, Russia and Peru. During the course of these projects, we have engaged in critical discussion of international schooling, which has helped to develop my own thinking. I would like to acknowledge the contribution made by all of the colleagues who participated in the collaborative research studies, especially Jane Medwell, Lucy Cooker, Mark Gibson and Howard Stevenson.

Being 'international' is now used in many countries as a unique selling point for schools competing for students in both the state and private sectors (Brooks & Waters, 2015). At the same time, international comparisons such as PISA (the Programme for International Student Assessment) are now dominating evaluation of state education policies in many countries (Niemann, Martens & Teltemann, 2017). Universities are also eager to advertise themselves as international, a trend that manifests itself both in Western universities opening overseas campuses and in non-Western universities seeking the prestige attached to the label 'international' (Evison, Bailey, Taylor & Tubpun, 2019). In other words, the concept of being international no longer only resides in international schools themselves but, having incubated there, is now reaching its tentacles across wider systems of education. These factors mean that it is increasingly important to understand how being 'international' is conceptualized in diverse cultural settings. Despite these differences, this book shows that, like the elite schools of the past, international schools are creating their own shared identities of students, as part of what can be seen as an emerging 'class-for-itself' (Bunnell, 2010). Alongside this, we will see how teachers and leaders working in these schools differ from those working in national systems of education (Tarc & Mishra Tarc, 2015).

International schools and international schooling already dominate global politics at the time of writing. Boris Johnson, Prime Minister of the UK, received his early education at the European School of Brussels, where he met his first wife. Justin Trudeau, Prime Minister of Canada, is a graduate of an International Baccalaureate programme at his school in Quebec. Kim Jong-Un, the Supreme Leader of North Korea, was schooled in Switzerland, although it is unclear which school he attended. However, aside from these high-profile examples, perhaps of more interest is the way in which international schools are now educating a growing proportion of the global middle class in many countries. Across much of Asia, the journalists, lawyers, doctors, engineers, academics and executives of the next twenty years are, at this moment, being educated in international schools.

This book seeks to understand the positioning, power and future potential of international schools.

1

Globalization, Education and the International Schools Movement

Introducing International Schools

International schools are key sites in which globalization is contested and enacted; however, they continue to receive insufficient attention from sociologists of education. Central concepts such as power, inequality, authority and identity continue to be debated primarily by reference to national systems of schooling, and it is necessary to complement such approaches with an examination of how these concepts can be operationalized in international terms (Brown & Lauder, 2011). International schools are places in which competing conceptualizations of globalization jostle for dominance: the idealistic vision of promoting social change coexists with the market pressure to attract affluent students, and the vision of holistic education for international-mindedness coexists with a narrower academic focus on gaining entry to elite universities. An exploration of how globalization impacts on different areas of school life and a sociological exploration of the implications for national systems of education is the focus throughout this book.

The origins of international schooling are contested. As early as the second half of the nineteenth century, economic and social change had led to an increasing concern with international understanding in Western societies, and some would claim that the first international school was three sister schools founded in England, Germany and France in the 1860s, whose students were to spend time studying in each of the three locations to promote their knowledge of other countries. The International College at Spring Grove, the English counterpart, involved such luminaries as the author Charles Dickens, the politician Richard Cobden and the biologist Thomas Huxley (Hayden & Thompson, 2008; Gardner McTaggart, 2018b). From the start, international schooling was the preserve of the aspirational and ideologically focused middle class.

Others see the birth of international schooling in the development of institutions to serve expatriate families – the children of missionaries, diplomats and those serving the needs of expanding international trade. Although there were small numbers of these kinds of international schools in the first half of the twentieth century – Yokohama International School and the International School of Geneva were both founded in 1924 – it was the international mobility of families after the Second World War that spawned the growth of the international schools movement (Resnik, 2012a). Beginning in 1946, the US Department of Defence sponsored schools for dependents of those stationed overseas, whilst other schools operated under the auspices of the Department of State with the two departments eventually running 367 schools worldwide between them (Resnik, 2012a). In 1953, the first European School was founded in Luxembourg to serve employees of the European Coal and Steel Community, a forerunner of the European Union; by 2017, thirteen schools operated across Europe under the auspices of the European Union. Commercial organizations also became involved in the provision of international schools; for example, by the start of the twenty-first century, the Shell Company operated schools around the globe to allow families to accompany employees to remote locations. These disparate examples underpin one of the common drivers behind international schooling; in each case, international schooling was seen as a prerequisite for the globally mobile worker.

More ideological or idealistic motivators also underpinned a few international schools in these early incarnations of international schooling, and the teachers and leaders of these schools may see themselves as part of the 'movement' alluded to in this chapter's title. The first United World College (UWC) was the UWC Atlantic College in Wales, which opened in 1962 with the aim of fostering world peace and international understanding, and inspired by the ideas of the German educationalist Kurt Hahn; today, there are eighteen colleges operating in diverse parts of the world, attempting to bridge international divides (UWC, 2021). They offer scholarships to bring together young people from all over the world to be educated together. In the same decade that the UWC began, the International Baccalaureate Organisation (discussed further below) was set up to provide a curriculum and qualification for international schools with an avowed commitment to promoting international-mindedness in young people.

Since these early days, international schools have changed markedly and the appellation is fixed to increasingly diverse institutions. Charting the landscape of international schooling can never be an exact science (Bunnell, 2014). There are many reasons for this lack of clarity. The international schooling sector rests in no statutory domain that could define and regulate its boundaries. Rather, it straddles the full range of cultural, economic and social variety to be found across human societies. Moreover, the study of international schooling has arguably been normative rather than descriptive; the term is seen as affording a certain status and, for many, gestures at deeply held (but perhaps not clearly articulated) values. I discuss this further in the following chapters. For now, it suffices to say that the assignation of 'international school' status to an institution is contested not simply by academics (as is usual in any field of study), but also hotly debated by practitioners.

Despite this lack of clarity, there is widespread agreement that international schooling is expanding. In 2008, Hayden and Thompson described international schools as a 'well-kept secret' (p. 15); nowadays, there are few countries in which such a claim could be made. The statistics usually cited are those from ISC Research, which defines international schools as those offering education in English outside of an English-speaking country. This definition is problematic, excluding such institutions as Washington International School, an International Baccalaureate School in Washington, DC, with students from over 100 countries, serving the international community in the US capital. It would also exclude the many schools worldwide immersing English speakers in Spanish, French, Japanese and so on – it is not clear why the English language should be privileged in this manner. Conversely, it includes schools that do not meet many other criteria that have been suggested for being considered to be 'international', such as having a nationally diverse student and staffing body or having an internationally minded ethos; in fact, some of the institutions included may be little more language tuition centres. Despite these definitional difficulties, ISC Research's data offers clear evidence of rapid growth in international schooling over the past twenty years (ISC, 2020c). The numbers suggest 343 per cent increase in schools from 2000 to 2020, from 2,584 to 11,451. The same period has seen a 501 per cent increase in international school students (from 969,000 to 5.82m); a 516 per cent increase in staff (from 90,000 to 554,000); and a whopping 1019 per cent increase in fee income (from 4.9bn to $54.8bn). From being a niche sector serving a few, international schooling has become big business.

International schooling has not simply expanded; it has also changed its focus. Two key changes have been that most of this expansion has been located in Asia and that the increased numbers have drawn largely from host-country nationals (children attending international schools within their passport country) rather than from expatriates. I discuss both of these further below. The implications of these changes will be one of the themes of this book.

Resnik (2012a, b) argues that the expansion of international schooling – either through establishment of separate schools or by adoption of international curricula within state schools – constitutes a 'denationalisation' of education systems. Resnik (2012b) suggests that national education systems were 'the main tool for the creation of nation-states' and suggests that this centuries-long creative process is being rapidly dismantled in a few decades by the advent of 'international schooling' – which Resnik defines as both the creation of distinct international schools and the permeation of international curricula and qualifications into state institutions. In some cases, this has been explicitly fostered by governments; the Blair government in the UK encouraged the establishment of at least one IB school in every school district. Similarly, the US Department of Education has funded a shift to IB education, particularly by schools serving large numbers of low-income children (Resnik, 2012a). In Australia, instituting international tracks has been used by some schools as a means by which to attract middle-class students.

Bunnell (2014) argues that the changes in both the scale and nature of international schooling mean that the established organizations (such as the Council of British International Schools) no longer 'represent' the field. He compares the earlier years (which he names the 'ideal' phase) to the contemporary situation (which he terms the 'post-ideal' phase), arguing that the ideal phase was characterized by a blend of pragmatics with idealism, whereas now commercial motivations have come to dominate. Bunnell's division is problematic. Firstly, there was no golden age of international schooling in which ideals reigned supreme; the post-war expansion of international schooling was, as we have seen, largely driven by the employment needs of large organizations and corporations, although the schools themselves were often parent-run rather than set up on a commercial footing. Secondly, the post-war international school was dominated by Westerners, both numerically and culturally, which means that its internationalism can be questioned. Arguably, through this rapid expansion, we have also seen the democratization and internationalization of international education, as non-Western players (school owners, parents, students and teachers) now have greater influence vis-à-vis the organizations who pioneered international schooling.

The relationship between these changes and social inequalities is another theme of this book. The expansion of international schooling has also been a commercialization of international schooling, and this has led to a shift in who the key decision makers are. In the new world of international schooling, the educational professional no longer dominates by default. Many new international schools are established by organizations or individuals without any background in education, and the IB itself no longer automatically turns to an educationalist for its Director General. It is unclear what the impact of these changing key players will be on inequalities within international schools.

These changes will not necessarily be for the worse. Some inequalities may be challenged by new international schools. It would be a simplification to say that any teacher can teach in the elite international schools of Asia; however, class signifiers such as accent, school, university and recreational pursuits simply do not have the same meaning in these cultural settings. Contrasting the websites of three branches of Dulwich College, the English public school founded in 1619 which has lately started opening international campuses illustrates this. Dulwich College England introduces its Master on its website; he has a doctorate; he previously worked at Eton; and outside of school he is a playwright, librettists and a Fellow of the Royal Society of Arts. By contrast, the Headmaster of Dulwich College Beijing places emphasis on sporting interests and his background in teaching in international contexts, whilst mentioning that he is currently studying for an MA. Similarly, the headteacher of Dulwich College Suzhou is interested in travel and is currently studying for an EdD; his background is teaching in state schools in Australia. The cultural capital being signalled by these potted biographies differs significantly. Being white and male seems to matter in representations of international school leadership in Asia (Gibson & Bailey, forthcoming); being upper middle class and highly educated matters more for public school leadership in the UK. Whilst there may be a class levelling in international schools, conversely, ethnicity may have a greater prominence. The demand for native English-speaking teachers may in practice be equated with white and Western English-speaking teachers (Tarc et al., 2019). The relationship between international schools and social inequalities will be explored in Chapter 7.

The International Baccalaureate

The changing world of international world is perhaps best exemplified by examining the history of the International Baccalaureate Organization, which was initially established to offer an international qualification for the graduates of international schools. The International School of Geneva and the UWC

Atlantic College (based in South Wales) were both instrumental in the initial development of its diploma for international schools in the early 1960s, although these efforts were not crystallized in the formal founding of the IBO (later rebranded as the IB) until 1968. The origins of the programme were therefore grounded in the needs of Northern European international schools.

Originally focused on developing a school-leaver qualification and attendant courses of study, termed the Diploma Programme (DP), the IB has subsequently developed programmes for other levels of schooling. The Middle Years Programme (MYP) was launched in 1994, whilst the Primary Years Programme (PYP) was introduced from 1997. More recently, the IB responded to criticism that the diploma only meets the needs of the most academic students by launching the Career Related Programme (CP) in 2012. Initially, the IB programmes could only be studied in English or French; Spanish was added as a third language in 1984. In discussion below of the 'curriculum' in IB schools, it is acknowledged that there are multiple programmes; however, there are common curricula components across these programmes, specifically a focus on developing international-mindedness and the attributes of the IB's Learner Profile (discussed further in Chapter 2).

The IB is now a major international organization with extensive brand recognition outside international school circles. It is usually equated to its diploma programme in the public imagination, which has become seen as a 'gold standard' for education systems worldwide. The diploma is a recognized qualification for university admission across most Western systems of education. Whilst its assessment centre remains in Wales and it still has an office in Switzerland, its three 'global centres' are based in The Hague, Singapore and Washington, DC. The IB is proud of its global reach, noting that by the end of 2019 its programmes were offered in 157 countries, across 5,175 schools. However, the allegation that it is a predominantly Western organization has dogged the IB since the outset. In the United States alone, 1855 schools offer at least one IB programme, representing over 1/3 of IB schools worldwide. In addition, the programmes themselves have often been criticized for their implicitly Western values (Hill, 2006).

The IB's original focus on meeting the needs of international schools has changed over the years. Instead of expanding in the international schools market alone, the IB has focused on developing government partnerships, and its programmes are now developed in many government schools, including in the United States, Australia, Canada, Ecuador and Malaysia. Conversely, it is unclear whether it continues to address international school needs; by 2013, only 23 per cent of international schools were using IB programmes whilst approximately 43 per cent were using other international curricula such as the International Primary Curriculum (IPC) (Bunnell, 2014). Moreover, the current situation is that the majority of international schools have their students working towards British qualifications rather than international qualifications or those from any other country (Bunnell, 2019).

The IB is a not-for-profit organization. However, in 2003 it opened the IB Fund, which is incorporated in the United States, for its organizational fund-raising, and since 2008 it has been registered as a limited company in the UK. The IB's total revenue for the year ending June 2019 was US$ 247.5m (IB, 2020b). This is drawn from fees from schools, as well as professional development, assessment and publications; becoming an IB school is a major financial commitment for a school (Resnik, 2012b). In addition, the IB receives donations from individuals and, on occasion, receives government funding for specific initiatives.

Resnik (2012b) argues that the shifting orientation of the IB is reflected in the changing backgrounds of its Director General. The founding director was Alec Peterson, who had previously worked as a headteacher and was concurrently a professor at the University of Oxford. At the time that Resnik wrote her work, the Director General was Jeffrey R. Beard, who had come to the IB from the world of business. The Director General at the time of writing (2020) is Dr Siva Kumari, the first woman and the first Asian to hold the position, who had previously led the Asia-Pacific branch of the IB. Through this changing leadership, we can see the shifting focus of the IB reflected. The future direction of the IB may be signalled through the appointment of Dr Kumari's replacement, which has been announced to take place in early 2021.

Diversity in International Schooling

As the world of international schooling has expanded, it has – perhaps inevitably – become more diverse. Consequently, there have been several attempts by researchers both to demarcate its boundaries and to categorize different types of international schools. As we shall see in this chapter, the fluid and rapidly evolving nature of the sector has meant that these efforts have not always been successful.

The definition of an international school is widely contested, and every research article on the subject now begins with a bow to this difficulty before carrying on with an analysis regardless. There are many potential ways in which the definition could be settled – by appeal to authority, as residing in self-identity of each institution, or by some agreed set of criteria established by researchers. In each of these possible respects, the essence of international schooling has escaped being captured. First, the appeal to authority is doomed to failure as there is no clear authority able to judge this area; in Malaysia, an international school is clearly defined by the Malaysian government as a school that is not following the Malaysian curriculum. Such a definition might cause problems in the United States, where there are hundreds of state schools using the programmes of the International Baccalaureate. As noted above, ISC Research, the major organization collecting statistics on the sector, defines an international school as a school providing English-medium education outside of an English-speaking country, but this is a definition riddled with difficulties. The Council of International Schools, on the other hand, is more concerned with the ethos of the schools and whether it promotes the skills needed for students to become 'global citizens' (CIS, 2020); this sounds like a possible solution until one remembers that the OECD has recently announced that ALL students worldwide should be assessed on their global competence (Ledger et al., 2019).

A second approach might be to acknowledge a school as international if it chooses to call itself such. The problem with this approach is that in some contexts being seen as international is high status and consequently thought to give competitive advantage in the market for students and parents. The use of the title 'international' may therefore be seen as a marketing device – albeit one that gestures at a wider discourse that merits investigation – rather than indicating anything about the nature of the schooling received. As a result, whilst many researchers accept self-definition in selecting schools for study, they may wish to supplement this by establishing criteria for categorizing the diverse group of self-proclaimed international schools.

Let us, then, examine attempts by researchers to define and categorize international schools. Hayden and Thompson (2013) have proposed a typology that divides the sector into three types. Type A traditional international schools serve the children of globally mobile parents, such as the offspring of diplomats, missionaries or international businessmen. Type B ideological international schools have a commitment to education for global peace or understanding, exemplified by Kurt Hahn's United World Colleges. Hayden and Thompson argue that these two types of international schooling are now joined by a third category, the rapidly growing Type C non-traditional school.

The Type C school was originally defined by Hayden and Thompson (2013) in terms of its student body – it mostly enrols its pupils from the socio-economic elite of the host country rather than from globally mobile expatriates. However, Hayden and Thompson also note that a Type C school is often situated in a developing country. Subsequently, other theorists (such as Bunnell, Fertig & James, 2016) have argued that Type C schools are typically privately owned and are therefore more commercial in nature.

It is hard to avoid the overtone of disdain that many commentators employ when referring to the growth of Type C international schooling. Some commentators have questioned whether these constitute 'legitimate' international schools (Bunnell, Fertig & James, 2016), and see Type A and Type B schools as the true bearers of the label. It is sometimes unclear whether it is the aspirational nature of Type C international schooling that invites this contempt (they are institutions for the newly arrived middle class of developing countries in Asia) or the for-profit nature of many Type C schools. However, it should be noted that international schools have always been middle-class institutions and that profit motivations clearly underpinned many Type A schools, such as the schools run by the Shell Corporation.

The Changing Market for International Schools

Hayden and Thompson's (2013) typology focuses on how to characterize individual schools. Equally important is to understand the changing environment in which these schools are operating. This growth of this significant sector of education is largely unregulated. Although national governments each have some oversight in the legal processes required to set up a school in their country, and although some international schools have banded together and established forms of international accreditation (the Council for International Schools, British Schools Overseas and schools registered to deliver the programmes of the IBO being notable examples), the market for international education remains uncoordinated, uncontrolled and unregulated. This unregulated market is rapidly evolving, as a result of both demand and supply side changes in the provision of international schools.

Demand side changes for international schooling are many. Keeling (2012) argues that international schools are now dominated by locals – with approximately 80 per cent of their students coming from the host country and only 20 per cent from expatriate families – a complete reversal of the situation thirty years earlier. This growth of host country families using international schools is attributable to several factors – which differ across different sociocultural contexts. Many countries have seen a relaxation of government restrictions on host country children attending international schools. For example, in Malaysia, Malaysian students were not able to enrol in international schools until 2006. Between 2006 and 2011, schools were capped at no more than 40 per cent of a school's enrolment. Since 2012, that cap has been lifted, and the number of international schools in the country has grown and local students now account for over 50 per cent of international school enrolment. However, it should be noted that within the country's market for international schools, there remain schools that are, in practice, exclusively local and others that are dominated by expatriates. The growth in global demand international schooling has not been a homogeneous phenomenon. As noted above, previous commentators have pointed to a greater growth in Asia than in other parts of the world. The growth of the Asian middle class has made a large contribution to this demand, and is explored in Chapter 2.

Alongside these demand side changes in who is seeking international schooling, there has been attendant supply side change. The expansion in international schooling means that there are now fewer locales in which there is a monopoly international schooling provider – instead, the market is becoming stratified with a range of schools offering international schooling at markedly different prices to meet the needs of different sub-markets. Moreover, rather than these schools being run by parents or established as charitable organizations, the expanding demand has encouraged the entry of for-profit organizations into the international school world. There is an increasing number of schools being run by powerful corporations operating a chain of schools across many countries, or even continents.

Waterson (2016) notes this rise in for-profit international education, noting that whilst twenty years earlier hardly any international schools were profit-seeking, at the time of Waterson's writing approximately 2/3 were for-profit. Waterson notes that the idea of 'profit' in international schooling might be contested by the owners of these schools, who often see themselves as social entrepreneurs who would reinvest profits in the schools themselves. Nevertheless, this is a significant shift in the ownership and incentive structures of people operating schools in this sector. Waterson raises the question of whether this will change the nature of international schooling, with a possible move away from idealistic conceptions of international education as commercial interests come to dominate. In particular, he focuses on the growing numbers of foreign-owned firms operating a number of international schools, in other words the way in which international schooling is increasingly becoming the preserve of transnational corporations.

This 'corporatisation of international schooling' (Waterson, 2016) raises a number of potential concerns. Trans-National Corporations (TNCs) have very limited loyalty to the individual countries in which they are operating, and can scarcely be expected to pay attention to the impact of their operations on local labour markets, for example. Their economics of scale may make it challenging for smaller schools to operate in the market, and they may exert an influence over textbook publishers and professional development providers as a result of their market dominance. Overall, then, the rise of TNCs in education presents a potential erosion of the power of state actors and collective decision-making over education (Waterson, 2016). Waterson expresses concern that commercial interests will affect quality and crowd out other ways of conceptualizing education. We examine the impact of ownership on the principals of international schools in Chapter 3.

Although Waterson noted that only a small minority of international schools were owned by TNCs, their market infiltration has continued unabated since Waterson was writing – with an over 50 per cent growth in the Nord Anglia chain alone (see the example of Nord Anglia below). In addition, a new phenomenon has risen to dominance – the exporting of public school schooling from the West. A number of prestige private schools from the United States, Canada and the UK have opened overseas campuses run on for-profit lines, either directly operated by the home school or on a franchise basis. Dulwich, Marlborough and Epsom are elite boarding schools from the UK who now have Asian off-shoots. Branksome Hall, a prestigious independent girls' school from Ontario, founded in 1912, opened a campus in South Korea in 2012. Bunnell, Courtois and Donnelly (2020) chart the expansion of British public schools offering overseas campuses, arguing that there is broadening their geographic spread, but still largely focused on the Middle East and South East Asia; they suggest that this is an example of the increasing diversification and intensification of competition in the global market for education, and that new modes of legitimation of being sought to retain competitive advantage.

It is worth re-emphasizing that the international schools market varies markedly country by country, and cannot be seen as a single, homogenous entity. International schools do not spread uniformly across a continent. Egypt has – both in numbers of schools and numbers of students – nearly 90 per cent of the international schools market in North Africa. In some countries there is a far stronger tradition of using private schooling – of which international schooling is a part – than in others. In Dubai, for example, more Emirati parents now choose to send their children to private schools (usually English medium) than to public ones (Azzam, 2019).

Although Europe has seen growth in the international school sector, it is nowhere near to matching the rate of expansion that has been seen across most of Asia. Moreover, European international schools do not adhere to the trend towards dominance by British qualifications. Having said that, European international schools do not only follow the IB programmes either. Fifty years ago, it was a European International School – the International School of Geneva – that spearheaded development of the IB Diploma. In more recent years, international curriculum innovation has again been led by a European international school, with the Common Ground Collaborative being born out of work at the International School of Brussels under the directorship of Kevin Bartlett.

An alternative typology of international schooling that seeks to capture these changes in governance and their implications for school leadership has been proposed by James and Sheppard (2014). They argue that schools should firstly be contrasted in terms of their ownership, which may be either private or community ownership. Second, they draw a distinction as to the purpose of the owners, between for-profit and not-for-profit focused organizations. In combination, these two dimensions lead to four possibilities for ownership:

1. Private for-profit
2. Private not-for-profit
3. Community for-profit
4. Community not-for-profit

They concede that the third category – a school that is community owned but seeking to make a profit – is uncommon and that they found no examples of such a school in their extensive survey of international school leaders. They demonstrate how the different categories of governance impact upon the day-to-day leadership and operation of the school.

Typologies can be problematic. They risk reducing the complexity of a school to a single essence, when in fact institutions evolve and contain stakeholders with conflicting beliefs about their purpose. Despite this, typologies are helpful in identifying essential differences, whilst recognizing that specific institutions will never conform to such neat categories. Hayden and Thompson's (2008) typology of international schools and James and

Sheppard's (2014) more recent analysis of types of international school governance both demonstrate how the nature and purpose of international schools have evolved since their origins in mid-twentieth century society. The need to write such typologies has emerged as a response to increasing contestation in what constitutes the key elements of international schooling, and changes in the range of institutions on offer.

This changing world of international schooling can be illustrated by firstly examining the rise of a three contrasting transnational corporations in international schooling (Nord Anglia Education, The Taylors Group and Dulwich College International), and secondly by describing the evolving international school market in one specific country (China).

Example: Nord Anglia Education

Nord Anglia Education is a major for-profit player in the international school world. At the time of writing, Nord Anglia owns sixty-six international schools in twenty-nine countries (Nord Anglia Education, 2020). This is not just big business, but enormous business; Nord Anglia Education Inc was acquired by Bach Finance Limited in 2017 for approximately US$4.3 billion (Badkar, 2017; DNB, 2020).

The organization was originally set up in 1972 to teach English as a foreign language, and the company has always maintained a broadly educational remit, although its main focus has changed over time. For example, it was a key player in day-care provision in England in the 1990s. Nord Anglia moved into international schooling in the early years of the twenty-first century, and by 2008 had sold off its other interests in order to focus exclusively on international schools. The chain has a history of buying up existing international schools; for example, in 2017 it bought seven schools from the British Schools Foundation. Its headquarters were originally in London, although it moved to Hong Kong for a six-year stint from 2012 (Atack, 2018) – at the time, it explained that it wanted to focus on its global interests – before returning to London again.

The Nord Anglia Advisory Board is chaired by Lord David Puttnam, probably better known to the general public as the producer of such films as *Chariots of Fire* and *Bugsy Malone*. Other board members include academics from other the world, firmly establishing Nord Anglia's serious educational credentials. However, real leadership comes from a more commercial perspective, under the Chief Executive Andrew Fitzmaurice, whose background is decidedly non-educational with positions at EasyCar.com and TNT Express UK featuring in his biography (Nord Anglia Education, 2020).

Nord Anglia schools are usually positioned as high-end international schools. For example, its Collège du Léman in Switzerland featured seventh on *The Telegraph*'s (2016) ranking of '[t]he world's most exclusive boarding schools', with fees just under £70,000 per annum. Some schools offer IB programmes; others follow the English National Curriculum, the French Baccalaureate or offer US Advanced Placement classes.

Example: The Taylor's Group

Taylor's Education Group exemplifies a second kind of for-profit chain found within international schooling, being regional rather than global in reach. This is a Malaysia-based company and nearly all of its educational holdings are in Malaysia where it holds a college, a university and six international schools (it also has a university in Vietnam and an international school in Singapore). It clearly does not have the global spread of Nord Anglia Education, nor do its schools necessarily seek the same premium end of the market. Rather, Taylor's group has carefully differentiated its schools within a smaller geographical area so that they are not competing with one another, but are targeted at different niche markets. It has three schools in or just outside KL, one of which offers an Australian curriculum, whilst the other two have contrasting fee structures; the fee for Year 13 at Taylor's School is MYR 15,230, whereas at Garden International School the same year group is more than twice as expensive at MYR 32,370.

Example: Dulwich College International

A third type of transnational chain of international schools is the establishment of overseas campuses by prestigious Western schools. A number of English public schools (the most elite category of private school) and other prestigious Western schools such as Ontario's Branksome Hall now operate campuses across China.

For example, Dulwich College, which was founded in 1619, has campuses in South Korea, Singapore and Myanmar, as well as four China campuses. It proudly describes this collection of international campuses as '[t]he Dulwich Commonwealth of Schools' on its website (Dulwich College, 2020), seemingly oblivious to the postcolonial connotations of the term 'Commonwealth'. The original Dulwich College in the UK describes these campuses in terms of the educational opportunities that they offer to its British students, with opportunities to visit China for language, sport and music development. The website proclaims that '[t]he college also derives a regular income from our partnership operations with no capital investment of its own'. Again, the postcolonial overtones are salient.

The nature of 'English public schooling' abroad is therefore qualitatively different from English-based public schooling. Institutions such as Dulwich College were set up to educate poor scholars and have retained charitable status over the centuries. Dulwich College's mission – publicly available on the list of registered charities – continues to be exclusively educational. By contrast, Dulwich International seeks to make a profit, both for the original College and for its investors; for example, Dulwich College Yangon received a capital investment of US$30 million from Yoma Strategic Holdings (Dulwich College International, 2016), a corporation that has a diverse list of business interests, including real estate, financial holdings and automotive and heavy equipment. In other words, the two Yangon campuses are part of property developments in the city with education being just one element of the package that prospective buyers want from a new residential estate.

Example: China

In 2018–19, there were 857 English-medium international schools in China – that is, 8.3 per cent of the global total – educating just over 370,000 students with total annual tuition fees approximately USD 3.92 billion (ISC Research, 2019a). This enormous market is dominated by powerful international school companies that operate groups of schools; in 2018–19, there were twelve companies that operated more than eight schools apiece with the largest operating thirty-nine schools (that is, approximately 4.6 per cent of all international schools in China (ISC Research, 2019a)). Most of these schools are concentrated in large metropolitan areas; in 2019, Beijing alone had 151 international schools, whilst Shanghai had 168 (ISC Research, 2019b).

The majority of these schools were Chinese owned (ISC Research, 2019a), but an increasing number of prestigious UK and US private school brands have opened schools in China. By 2019, there were forty-seven Chinese campuses of British schools, usually highly prestigious English public schools; these included, for example, three campuses of Wellington College and the four campuses of Dulwich College (Turner, 2019). News reports claimed that the Chinese government had got 'fed up' with British private schools taking the best students out of government schools (Turner, 2019).

Overview of This Book

What, then, is international schooling? Is it a movement, as suggested in the title of this chapter, with diverse individuals and institutions together constituting a loose network working for social change? Is it a sector of education, a set of institutions with specific functions within the educational system of a particular country of geographical region? Is it a market, governed by the vagaries of supply and demand as the global economy changes? This chapter has problematized the nature of international schooling and shown how each of these ways of analysing the history of international schooling may contribute to our understanding of their growth.

This introductory chapter has raised the main themes that are explored in more depth through the remainder of this volume. This analysis underpins the discussion throughout, but the focus of each chapter will be different. Chapter 2 continues the perspective of this first chapter by introducing key theoretical lenses that have dominated the analysis of international schooling. I will examine globalization in more depth, discuss competing ideologies of international schooling and critically examine how international schools can be conceptualized.

Chapters 3–6 then look inside international schools to understand and analyse their micropolitics. In Chapter 3, I consider the micropolitics of international schooling, identifying how some of the changes described in this chapter impact on the micropolitics of international schools, as seen from the perspective of school principals. In Chapter 4, I shift my attention from school leaders to the teachers, and introduce a range of theoretical lenses for understanding the identity and professional practices of international school educators. In Chapter 5, I look at what happens within the classroom itself, to understand how pedagogical practices are effected by the linguistic, social and economic contexts in which international schools are operating. Chapter 6 then asks to what extent social and cultural inequalities may be reproduced through the curriculum of an international school.

In Chapters 7 and 8, the insights from earlier chapters are used to consider the evolving systemic effects of international schooling on global inequalities. Chapter 7 examines the ways in which international schools may both exacerbate and ameliorate social inequalities. Chapter 8 draws together the arguments from across the chapters to suggest that more attention needs to be paid to theorizing international education; in this chapter, I theorize that international schools are a key site for the replication of global inequalities, and that as new forms of inequality emerge their position on the stage of globalization merits far more detailed examination. Finally, I summarize the main arguments of the book in the final chapter, looking ahead to possible future changes in international schooling.

Throughout, this book does not report systematically on a particular piece of research, although its argument is informed by the multiple research projects on international schooling that I have undertaken with my colleagues over a period of many years. These various studies, some commissioned by the International Baccalaureate to evaluate aspects of its programmes and some independent studies into particular aspects of international schooling funded by our universities, have enabled us systematically to study international schools in disparate cultural settings. We have conducted surveys, interviews and focus groups with parents, students, school leaders and sometimes, policymakers and programme developers. We have collected data in Bahrain, Malaysia, China, Indonesia, Singapore, Thailand, the UK, the United States, Russia, Spain, Kenya and Mexico. I do not have space systematically to report on all of these studies in this volume; the methods of data collection and data analysis have been reported elsewhere. However, throughout the book, I draw on these multiple data sets by including ground-level analysis through intimate vignettes (Kenway & Fahey, 2009; Tarc & Mishra Tarc, 2015). As Kenway and Fahey (2009) suggest, narratives enable us to illuminate the shadows of globalization.

Throughout this book, we will continue to see that the expansion of international schooling is both a reflection of profound economic and social change, may be used by government as a means of social engineering and is a fascinating phenomenon worthy of study in its own right.

2

Conceptualizing the International School

Introduction

The preceding chapter described changes in the world of international schooling; this chapter begins the work of analysing them. I argue that increasing globalization of economies has created an expanding catchment of the Global Middle Class (GMC), a disparate group incorporating both globally mobile executives of multinationals, and the expanded host-country middle class seeking to enrol their children in international schools. I look at the ways in which this group reproduces itself, with attention to the particular role played by education. As part of this discussion, I introduce key ideas such as cultural capital, which will recur in subsequent chapters. Alongside these changes in demand for international schools, globalization has also resulted in the supply-side changes in the market for international schooling we have already discussed – most notably the emergence of chains of international schools and the establishment of satellite campuses of prestigious UK and US private schools, especially in Asia. I introduce the idea of discourse and the construction of the social and institutional identities as a further key idea to consider in analysing international schooling.

The focus on this chapter is on the conceptual framework rather than empirical analysis. The systematic application of these concepts to specific aspects of international schooling is the work of later chapters.

Globalization

Throughout this book, I will argue that international schools exemplify some of the social and economic changes wrought by globalization. However, the relationship between international schools and globalization is complex. There are many ways of understanding globalization, some of which focus on different types of change that have been wrought in the contemporary world and others looking at the ideologies concerning such change.

Globalization is a multifaceted phenomenon, referring to the increasing connectedness between different parts of the world. It refers to the tightening networks across the globe that underpin economic life, social connections and cultural activities, and the consequent international aspects of how we are governed. Globalization incorporates flows of goods, people and technologies. Globalization additionally refers to interdependence between different people and places, but in some cases interdependence actually constitutes dependence, as globalized relationships may be forms of dominance.

Globalization should not, then, be confused simply with international trade. Globalization includes, but is not limited to, the increased integration of the world economy (Olssen, 2004). It is not a qualitatively new phenomenon, since there has been integration within the global economy since before the First World War (and of course international trade has been around for millennia). Rather, globalization refers to an acceleration in these developments within social, cultural, economic and political life, rather than to an entirely new process (Olssen, 2004).

Globalization is sometimes confused with a neoliberal dominance of the free market in international affairs, but the definition above includes no ideological commitment to marketization. Indeed, Olssen (2004) distinguishes between two distinct forms of globalization – the first is the increased connectiveness facilitated by new developments in communication, capital movement, technology and transportation, whilst the other refers to the processes of deregulation, privatization and liberalization that have taken place in the international economy. Yet, whilst there are progressive forms of globalization, it is true that a neoliberal market ideology has sometimes been the dominant ideology in globalization of education (Zajda, 2020). This perhaps explains why Cambridge and Thompson (2001) distinguish between internationalism, which they define as a concern with the relationship between nations, and globalization, which they see as an ideology promoting the expansion of free market capitalism. They suggest that these two suggest different ways of understanding international schooling. They use the 'melting pot' as a metaphor to describe international schooling according to the first ideology, and 'a big Mac and a Coke' as a metaphor to describe globalized international schooling according to the second. By contrast, in this book, I do not equate globalization with neoliberal economic change, although we will see that the current dominant form of globalization is indeed heavily influenced by neoliberal ideology.

Neither does globalization necessarily mean homogenization. Although some theorists have been quick to proclaim 'the end of history', assuming both that Western liberal values are coming to dominate (Fukuyama, 1992) and that humankind is progressing towards a better future (these two very different assumptions are sometimes conflated), there is ample evidence of persisting divergence and ongoing cultural conflict. 'Glocalization' is a term that has been coined in the last thirty years to describe how widespread approaches may be adapted for specific places. The expression has been attributed to the development of commercial practices in Japan, where international business strategies were adjusted to fit Japanese culture, although this may be an urban myth (Roudometof, 2016a). Some theorists have critiqued the idea of glocalization, pointing out that the global can only ever exist in specific instantiations and therefore that all globalization is necessarily glocalization, but this rests on the assumption that globalization somehow produces difference (Roudometof, 2016b).

There are, then, two conflicting views of globalization. For some theorists, globalization incorporates a tendency to homogenize – more specifically, a Eurocentric narrative of globalization may be seen as the nature of globalization per se. For others, globalization rests on difference; indeed, economists have offered some support for this latter view – for instance, Olivier, Thoenig and Verdier (2008) have demonstrated that, under certain conditions, the integration of goods markets can actually stimulate cultural divergence rather than convergence as sellers seek to establish a market niche. Globalization is, then, a contested phenomenon, but nevertheless one that points to important economic and social changes in the contemporary world.

There is an extensive literature on globalization in education (Olssen, 2004), mostly focused on international aspects of higher education or the internationalization of national systems of education (Hayden, 2011). Some of the interest in educational globalization stems from the market opportunities offered by educational migration. The connection between education and migration is complex, incorporating groups as diverse as international university students, and refugees and asylum seekers; Newman, Hoechner and Sancho (2020) point to the diverse groups receiving education in international contexts and differing in their construction of what it means to be an 'educated' person. However, educational globalizations do not necessarily relate to movement of either students or educators. Bates (2011a) points to the increasing wealth and power accruing to transnational corporations, and charts how this is reflected in education; for example, he points to the use of private provision to meet basic educational needs in developing countries, with powerful organizations such as the OECD and the WTO brokering educational trade. Bates (2011a) argues that international assessment mechanisms such as PISA are detaching educational decision-making from national authorities and reconstructing education as a commodified good that can be traded on the world stage.

I suggest that a pertinent example of Bates's thesis of the commodification of education is the 'GREAT' campaign launched by the British Department for International Trade in 2012 to build on the potential for promoting British goods and services offered by the London Olympics and the Queen's Diamond Jubilee. Emphasis was put on study opportunities offered by the UK, and the idea that 'Education is GREAT' was a major theme of the campaign. In other words, education was a commodity promoted in the same way as tourism, entertainment and industry (GREAT Britain Campaign, 2020).

The themes in this general literature on education and globalization are salient for international schooling. International schools are simultaneously precursors for globalization, originally founded to enable managers and executives to move globally, and also products of globalization, with different types of school emerging which reflect shifts in world markets. Furthermore, as we shall see, the changing form and function of international schooling are also connected to globalization. As a Eurocentric narrative of globalization comes to dominate world social and economic affairs, then I would predict that a Eurocentric understanding of international schooling would predominate as well. This will form a key argument in Chapters 5–7.

In summary, we can only understand the changes in the market for international schooling that were described in the previous chapter by analysing the global socio-economic changes that are occurring in the early twenty-first century. Throughout this book, I shall argue that the international schools have become a site in which this myriad of changes that are loosely grouped under the term 'globalization' can be evidenced and the conflicts which they threaten are enacted. In the next section, I exemplify this argument by considering the rise of the Global Middle Class (GMC) and its connection to international schooling.

The Growth of the Global Middle Class

In 2009, *The Economist* declared that 'for the first time in history more than half of the world is middle class' (Parker, 2009). Koo (2016) provides evidence that whilst the middle class is expanding globally, this growth is particularly rapid in emerging economies, especially in Asia. This is a heterogeneous class grouping; Buheji and Ahmed (2020) note that the middle class is disparate. They adopt a broad definition of the middle class, suggesting that it is those who are not poor in relation to their national poverty line. They define the middle class primarily in economic terms, but also note that the middle class have security in terms of housing, healthcare, education and other life opportunities, some of which they use to enable their children to access greater economic security in the next generation. Within this disparate class, there is a significant segment that is globally oriented in both employment and leisure, speaks English, and enjoys a Western style of life (Koo, 2016) – it is this group that is termed 'the Global Middle Class' (GMC).

These rising levels of affluence may be welcomed for many reasons – ranging from companies seeking a market to countries seeking political stability and democratization (Koo, 2016). Our interest here, however, is in their impact on education. *The Economist* argued that whilst the term 'middle-class' is imprecise and varies between different economic contexts, one common feature of the middle class is that they have sufficient income for discretionary spending; after paying for their essentials, they may choose to purchase a refrigerator, an overseas holiday or – the specific interest in this volume – education. Again, the GMC may be distinguished from other segments of the middle class because their patterns of consumption are globally oriented towards, say, travel or schooling their children to be globally competent.

The needs of the global middle class are connected to educational choices in multiple ways. Burrows (2015) has argued that in many places membership of this new middle class is overshadowed by the fear of slipping back into the dire poverty that remains a feature of many developing countries, suggesting that in Latin America, for example, almost 40 per cent of the middle class are at risk of losing their new status in response to economic fluctuations. In addition, Burrows (2015) suggests, there is a widespread perception that the quality of public education in many countries has not kept pace with their development in other respects. Hence, investment in restricted forms of education, such as international schooling and other forms of private education, is a way of buffering against the risks posed by economic insecurity. Similarly, focusing on the example of South Korea, Koo (2016) argues that this expansion has led to increasing divisions within the middle class, with individuals seeking class distinction, in part through conspicuous consumption and in part through education. Meanwhile, Ball and Nikita (2014) link educational choices by the GMC to identity-making; they argue that the GMC is a global service class, meeting the needs of transnational business, and that the 'global city' is the site of their choice-making in, for example, life-style, identity-making and education. Global mobility – although still restricted to a small minority – is now seen as a normal part of a middle-class career.

So where do international schools specifically fit into the new GMC's educational choices? Koo analyses the educational practices of the global middle class in South Korea, arguing:

> The dominant trend of educational change in Korea has been the twin development of privatization and globalization.
>
> (Koo, 2016: 447)

Koo exemplifies this through a discussion of the use of private tutoring and study-abroad programmes. Although Koo does not explicitly discuss international schools, the analysis offers insight into the rise of international schooling, not least because some of the study abroad sought by Korean parents takes place in international schools elsewhere in Asia, such as Singapore, Malaysia and the Philippines (De Guzman, Brown & Edwards, 2018).

The search for class advantage is not restricted to Asia, of course. In his analysis of the relationship between education and the labour market in Britain, Ware (2015) argues that the promise of social mobility through education in the twentieth and twenty-first centuries has been nothing more than a 'fraud'. As having better credentials became essential for the best jobs, a race to acquire these qualifications ensued, with increasing numbers of young people remaining in education and seeking ever-higher qualifications. As a result, there is now increased expenditure by families on efforts to get their children better credentials, at the same time as those same credentials lose value through credential inflation. As we have seen in Chapter 1, the international qualifications offered by the IB are increasingly sought by middle-class government schools in the United States, the UK and Australia.

Whilst recognizing Ware's argument that the middle class continue to experience precarity, it is clear that the Global Middle Class constitutes an elite, despite the nomenclature of being in the middle. The host-country nationals attending international schools in Asia may not be the high-flying international executives who peopled international schools in their earlier days, but their incomes and standard of living are high for developing nations. Buheji and Ahmed (2020) stress that attribution of class status must be relative to national norms, and by that measure the GMC is affluent. In the remainder of this book, I use terms such as 'advantage', 'elite' and 'privilege' to stress this relative status.

The Cultural Capital of the Global Middle Class

Many theorists have attempted to theorize the ways in which the GMC are able to reproduce and legitimate their class advantage, largely drawing on the work of Bourdieu (Bourdieu, 1986; Bourdieu, 1991) on different forms of capital. Bourdieu argued that there are many sorts of assets other than wealth which can be used to generate income and status. He argues that children internalize aesthetic preferences which give them 'Distinction' from other class groupings. They develop cultural capital, the competencies, skills and dispositions which give them access to particular positions, and social capital, through the networks of friends and acquaintances they can mobilize to achieve status and lucrative work. Their language skills also can be deployed as a way to distinguish them from others and therefore access power.

Several theorists have drawn on this approach to understanding advantage as they theorize the strategies that are specific to the Global Middle Class. The forms of cultural capital that have been claimed for members of the GMC in international schools (either students or teachers) include cosmopolitan capital, resilience capital (Poole, 2019b) and transition capital (Poole & Bunnell, 2020). I shall focus on exemplifying this in relation to cosmopolitan capital in this chapter.

International schools have a natural affinity with the economic needs of the new class strata of the Global Middle Class because they socialize students into cosmopolitanism. There is now a considerable literature exploring cosmopolitanism and its relation with social stratification (Kendall, Woodward & Skrbis, 2009; Ball & Nikita, 2014; Igarashi & Saito, 2014). Cosmopolitanism – a sense of feeling at home all over the world and being detached from more specific, local identities – meets the needs of globalized capital, which requires workers who are geographically mobile and can move fluidly between diverse contexts. Indeed, Poole and Bunnell (2020) argue that the distinguishing feature of the GMC, contrary to the middle class that is more geographically bound, is its possession of cosmopolitan capital – the skills and dispositions that enable individuals to move geographically with confidence. Cosmopolitanism is a form of cultural capital; it encapsulates the skills and dispositions that are required by the new Global Middle Class. As with any form of cultural capital, the question then becomes how education systems legitimate the advantage that accrues to that cultural capital through the values and the credentials that they offer. Public education systems have shifted their focus from a national outlook to a global approach, and it may be that this is partly connected to the rising emphasis on cosmopolitanism (Schumann, 2018). Beyond this, though, it can be argued that international schooling is intrinsically implicated in the reproduction of social class advantage through its valorization and credentialing of cosmopolitanism (Ball & Nikita, 2014; Wright & Lee, 2019) – the IB, for example, assesses students in part for their 'international-mindedness', a notion to which I return in Chapter 6.

The idea that international schooling fosters cosmopolitanism has been advanced both by those embracing it as a form of educational enrichment (e.g. Gunesch, 2015) and those critically analysing its role in the reproduction of social inequalities (e.g. Ball & Nikita, 2014). For example, Hayden (2012) analyses the mission statements of sixty-seven international schools to identify the extent to which these schools purported to be promoting cosmopolitanism, concluding that whilst their main focus was on academic and cognitive development, there was also a clear focus on developing the personal dispositions of the cosmopolitan. Similarly, Wright and Lee (2019) suggest that the International Baccalaureate Diploma facilitates a pathway from childhood into the global middle class through the cosmopolitan sensibilities and economic expectations that it fosters. They suggest that it offers a route for GMC parents to reproduce their class advantage and for less advantaged local families to find a route for their children into the GMC. Whilst their data are based exclusively on IB alumni studying at university in Hong Kong, the findings suggest a synergy between international schooling and the class positioning of the GMC.

As Ball and Nikita (2014) point out, school choice impacts on social class identity formation in two ways – it is both a way of expressing the identity of the parents making the choice and is a way of ensuring the future class identity of the children for whom that school choice is made. International schools reproduce the cosmopolitanism that is central to GMC identity by creating a flexible sense of citizenship whereby students feel removed from specific local identities but are able to blend into many others, and by offering access to global social networks. In other words, the identity constructed by international schooling enables the individual to respond easily to global market opportunities in the way that is demanded by borderless global capital:

> Global cities and international schools are social sites in which new kinds of class identity are formed and reproduced ... One key question then is whether the children of the global middle class are acquiring a new kind of post-national class

identity, and cosmopolitan sensibilities, through their education, and whether, together identity and sensibility are fostering a new kind of international surety and entitlement.

(Ball & Nikita, 2014: 88–9)

In addition to the role played by such forms of cultural capital, Bourdieu's theorizing enables us to consider other forms of advantage enjoyed by the GMC – specifically, can also be applied to the linguistic advantage enjoyed by the GMC attending international schools. Across much of Asia, international schooling equates to English-language education and is the means by which students develop the English-language fluency required for the cosmopolitan lifestyle described above.

However, this account of the GMC and the role played by international schooling in its reproduction is open to debate. For example, Brown and Lauder (2011) question whether there really is a homogeneous GMC requiring the same cosmopolitan capital to gain advantage across all cultural contexts; they suggest that such an account ignores the importance of national economic interests. This critique can be explored by more detailed analysis of the social relations of international schooling and their relationship to the social relations of the workplace.

The Social Relations of International Schooling

Another key approach for conceptualizing what happens to children during international schooling is the social relations of education. Rather than simply focusing on cosmopolitanism alone, this approach to analysing international education rests on a broader analysis of the curriculum and hidden curriculum of such institutions, and the kinds of behaviours to which they habituate their students.

The idea that there is a correspondence between the social relations of education and the social relations of capitalism was first propounded almost half a century ago by Bowles and Gintis (1976). Back in the 1970s, the extent of intergenerational transmission of income was doubted, with researchers asserting that within two to three generations any inequalities would even out. Moreover, the correlation between schooling and income was assumed to be a result of the impact that education has on cognitive ability. Bowles and

Gintis's (1976) evidence debunked this, and these days the idea that schooling develops non-cognitive routes to economic advantage is widely accepted. However, the details of their correspondence theory continue to offer insights into the intergenerational reproduction of advantage and have been updated by subsequent theorists.

Bowles and Gintis's (1976) seminal work contrasted schools serving middle-class and working-class neighbourhoods of the United States, noting that working-class schools and lower levels of schooling emphasized rote learning and obedience, had teacher-centred classrooms, and offered little learner autonomy, whereas middle-class schools and higher levels of education (such as post-compulsory education) offered students freedom to inquire, to question teacher autonomy and to take charge of their own learning. For Bowles and Gintis, the social relations of education were preparing working-class students to accept the powerlessness, tedium and repetition they would experience in working-class jobs, whereas middle-class students were being given the autonomy, the self-motivation, and the management skills they would require for middle-class careers. In other words, for Bowles and Gintis, the social relations of education played a key role in the reproduction of existing class inequalities through preparing students for the social relations they would later experience at work.

There have been many attempts to update Bowles and Gintis's seminal work. Back in the 1990s, I examined the UK's then newly introduced National Curriculum, arguing that it was no longer just preparing students for the social relations of employment but also for the social relations of consumption required in the post-Fordist economy (Bailey, 1995). Bowles and Gintis themselves revised their theory to allow for a less deterministic internalization of school norms and values (if all values are internalized, how does social change or protest ever occur?), and to allow for the importance of the norms and values of the home as well as those of school (Bowles & Gintis, 2002). In addition – and of specific interest to this volume – attempts have been made by some researchers to apply the theory to the social relations of international schools.

Resnik (2008) analyses the International Baccalaureate's Learner Profile, the ten character attributes that IB schools purport to develop across all of their programmes. She suggests that they match the qualities required to be an effective manager in a global corporation. Although the focus of the IB is ostensibly on the ideal global citizen, Resnik argues that this has become blurred with the ideal global worker. She argues that the social relations of international schooling mirror both the social relations of work and the social relations of consumption for the global elite.

Resnik (2008) suggests that key features that differentiate the modern global economy are flexibility, a focus on knowledge and information and the importance of networking. First, she argues that mass production has been replaced with customized production, and employers demand flexibility and multitasking from their employees. Second, she notes that many jobs now focus on information-processing activities rather than the manufacture of material things. Third, she posits that the new logic of interaction between both firms and individuals is networking – and therefore a premium is attached to the social capital that facilitates that. From these three key changes, she identifies a number of skills required by workers in this knowledge economy, such as problem-solving, critical thinking, self-reflection, the ability to apply knowledge, creativity and innovation, cognitive multiculturalism, continuous self-development and multitasking. Resnik demonstrates how these skills needed for the global knowledge economy are fostered by the IB programmes. Similarly, she looks at how the dispositions required by such employees also mirror those nurtured by the IB, such as adaptability, risk-taking and emotional multiculturalism. Finally, she argues that the forms of identity and abilities to work with others valorized by the IB – teamworking, networking and a sense of world citizenship – further contribute to the creation of an ideal global knowledge worker. Resnik's analysis is detailed and convincing, although it should be noted that her conclusions are based on textual analysis of the IB's claims for the characteristics of their graduates rather than looking at empirical data evidencing what actually happens in IB schools.

One theorist who does investigate this issue empirically is Lowe (2000), who explores the views of students completing different international qualifications – both IGCSEs and the IB Diploma. Lowe suggests that these students have been prepared for their place in companies operating internationally in the post-Fordist global economy. The students he surveys contrast the rote memorization they would have received in national systems of education with the all-round character education and emphasis on extracurricular activities of their international schools. Lowe suggests that students in these international schools are being given the attitudes and skills required to be a successful global worker; additionally, the students value international qualifications as certification of their fluency in English, the lingua franca of the globalized economy.

Despite such accounts supporting the idea of a correspondence between the social relations of international schooling and the social relations of work for members of the GMC, Brown and Lauder (2011) express reservations about this argument. Their reservations rest on a critique of the assumption that the GMC has homogeneity. Although, they suggest, the idea of a transnational middle class was plausible when Western neoliberalism dominated globalization, the recent rise of China and India makes this more questionable. Brown and Lauder (2011) suggest that we are not seeing the rise of a global ruling class, but instead of competition between different neo-empires. They point out that class formation in China cannot ignore the continued central role for the People's Party in deciding opportunities and therefore is very different to class formation in the West. They also suggest that some countries are using international schools to promote national competitive advantage in the global market place. In other words, Brown and Lauder argue for a more nuanced version of correspondence theory than any suggestion that a homogeneous global middle class is prepared for their common social relations of work through the social relations of international schooling.

Brown and Lauder distinguish between a class-in-itself – the common conditions and shared economic position experienced by individuals – and a class-for-itself – the awareness of shared interests. They argue that international schools may offer that shared consciousness and ideology, whilst also noting that the elite universities attended by their graduates may also contribute. However, this does not mean that the middle class of divergent nations truly have a shared economic position.

As a result, although Brown and Lauder's conclusion is that although there are extraordinary commonalities between the employee attributes that transnational corporations say they are seeking across diverse industries and different locations, and although these match the characteristics noted in Third Culture Kids attending international schools, they are reluctant to draw simplistically on correspondence theory, giving three reservations: first, drawing attention to the difficulty employers will have in identifying such skills; second, stressing that these skills may vary in their cultural interpretation; and third, arguing that recruitment is less dependent on actually possessing skills than on being able to manage the impression of doing so.

Moreover, since Brown and Lauder wrote their analysis, increasing numbers of countries have permitted their nationals to attend international schools in their passport country (the phenomenon of host-country nationals discussed in Chapter 1). In addition, the number of state schools adopting the programmes which were originally developed for international schools (such as the IB and the IPC) has risen. This suggests that national interests are in some ways served by international dimensions of schooling. This is in keeping with Brown and Lauder's conclusion that the middle class of nations such as China and India are not necessarily part of a homogeneous GMC with shared interests.

Brown and Lauder's critique is important, and the suggestion that international schools serve a homogeneous class across diverse nations yet somehow holding unified class interests is indeed problematic. However, the fact that the elites in the United States, India and China remain in competition with one another is compatible with the idea that there are sufficient shared features of the middle class across the world to justify the assertion that we are witnessing the emergence of a global educational phenomenon. Brown and Lauder's account offers a nuanced interpretation of global economic change and the HR needs of transnational corporations, but it needs to be complemented with data from within international schools themselves. I will briefly discuss one example to illustrate how such an analysis can be done.

Example: Correspondence Theory and Pro-social Learning

My work with my colleague Lucy Cooker on 'Caring' is one of the few studies to explore correspondence theory in international schooling empirically (Bailey & Cooker, 2018). Caring is one of the ten Learner Profile character attributes that featured in Resnik's (2008) documentary analysis discussed above. In our paper, we discuss the idea that there is a correspondence between the social relations of international schooling and the social relations of the global middle class through our analysis of prosocial character education in case-study IB schools in Austria, Thailand, Spain and Indonesia (see also Stevenson et al., 2015). We found that the case-study schools we visited placed an emphasis on the students' current and future social responsibilities to others. However, there was little mention of reciprocity in caring relationships; the students were primarily being prepared for one-way relationships in which they were caring for others less advantaged than themselves. In other words, the attitudes being instilled prepared them to be part of a global elite, albeit a compassionate one (Bailey & Cooker, 2018). In some schools, teachers spoke as if it was an achievement for their students to be caring despite their extremely wealthy backgrounds; it was clear that they believed there was a social chasm between the students and the recipients of their care. Caring was largely conceptualized in terms of generosity towards someone lower in the social order, a form of noblesse oblige. Students were made aware of social inequalities but for the purpose of learning leadership and benevolence rather than to challenge those inequalities. In summary, this form of prosocial education, as enacted in these case-study schools, reifies social inequalities, although we emphasize that this is not intrinsic to the curriculum, but is an effect of how it is enacted in the international contexts we visited.

Identity in International Schooling

In contrast to the structuralist concepts explored above, the final lens that I use in this volume for understanding international schooling draws on post-structuralism. The international-mindedness that is constructed in international schools can be understood as a technology of subjectification (Foucault, 1988). International schooling is, for its various stakeholders, a means of constructing the self. This applies to the leaders, the teachers, students and parents, and we shall see throughout this book how their relationship to international schooling – and to particular practices within international schooling – is a part of how they construct their identities. I shall examine, in particular, how international-mindedness (or similar discourses such as global competence) is understood as a way of being and behaving that is constructive of a particular identity (Ledger et al., 2019). Researchers have applied this post-structuralist approach to international schools in diverse ways. For instance, Adams and Fleer (2019) analyse the subjectivities constructed through the lunchtime social practices at one Middle Eastern international school, whereas Poole (2020b) uses a post-structuralist approach to understand international school teacher identity as constructed through ongoing dialogue. A post-structuralist approach to identity and subjectification reminds us that there is no single truth about international schooling, nor of the identities of students, teachers, and the schools themselves. Schools are not situated unproblematically, neither as internationally minded forces for social improvement nor as servants of a neoliberal world economic order, but are continually reconstructed through the behaviours of their participants.

Indeed, the many research activities which have contributed to this book have themselves constituted technologies of the self, as schools, students and teachers construct themselves through participation in research interviews, focus groups and surveys. According to Foucault (1988), such transformation enables the self to reach a higher state of happiness or perfection. Would that it were so!

Conclusion

This chapter has introduced a number of theoretical concepts that will recur in the chapters that follow. In the first two chapters of this book, I have delineated the evolving world of international schooling and shown how a range of tools may enable us to understand this. So far, I have considered these schools from the outside, as institutions. Having established this framework, it is now time for us to enter the international school. In the next chapter, I look at the organization and micropolitics of international schools.

3

The Micropolitics of International Schools

Introduction

Chapters 1 and 2 have focused on macro-aspects of the international school movement. This chapter shifts our focus to the micropolitics of the school – the struggles for scarce resources, control and power within the organization, in which the school leader plays a pivotal role (Ball, 1987). There is a focus on the messiness of 'doing' international schooling within institutions – how staff relationships are managed, how leadership is enacted and resisted, how individuals try to pursue their interests within organizational norms, how staffrooms can become Balkanized and whether contrived collegiality comes to dominate. The micropolitics of an international school may be thought to be particularly ripe for social conflict; the diversity of the staff and parent body, the isolation from the surrounding community and the high rates of transition that necessitate establishing consensus anew each academic year all may make the international school a particularly fraught environment (Caffyn, 2010). Our interest here is in how this messiness is resolved by school leaders in the context, as they attempt to lead a glocalized institution that reconciles pressures from the local context with global concerns.

Many commentators on international schooling have pointed to the leadership issues that are specific to international schooling. This chapter begins by describing some of these differences from leading a school in a national context. It then examines the evolving dominant forms of governance of international schools. Next, I analyse some of the specific challenges of balancing the local with the global that may be played out in an international school. I introduce case-studies, drawn from diverse settings, in order to hear how international school leaders talk about the micropolitics of their schools. The first example focuses on a school leader in Malaysia managing differing parental expectations of his role and parental involvement in education; the second explores the position of a school leader in China navigating competing stakeholder expectations of how an inquiry-based curriculum can be enacted; and the third examines a school leader in the UAE managing competing national and international regulatory frameworks. Critical analysis of these accounts reveals tensions between the language of internationalism and diversity, and the language of educational markets. I draw on this analysis to develop a critical conceptualization of micropolitics in an international context, focusing here on the perspectives of school principals. The voices of international school teachers, or other stakeholders in these organizations, do not feature in this chapter.

There is an expanding literature on leadership of international schools, though most has concentrated on describing its relationship with governance. I have already discussed shifting forms of governance in international schools in Chapter 1, and I touch on it again here. The primary focus here is on understanding the organizational cultures that are fostered in these schools from the perspective of their principals. Our main interest in this chapter is therefore on understanding how leaders of multicultural and multinational organizations navigate the blurred boundaries of their role, with competing conceptualizations of leadership, of effective governance, of legal frameworks and expectations existing within such diverse communities. I suggest that these leaders may feel an affective dissonance (Gibson & Bailey, forthcoming) between the commercial realities of their role and the educational beliefs into which they were professionally socialized (Bittencourt & Willetts, 2018).

The Micropolitics of Leading International Schools

In this section, we will consider the micropolitics of both becoming and being an international school principal. Little is known about *how* people become the principals of international schools (Bailey & Gibson, 2019). Since 1989, the Principals Training Center has offered leadership training courses and certification to educators in international schools. The IB has also recognized some IB leadership programmes offered by various universities worldwide. However, the extent to which such qualifications are pursued by those seeking senior leadership in international schools is unclear, as is the extent to which they meet the needs of such leaders.

Slightly more is known about *who* becomes an international school principal. Slough-Kuss (2014) reviews research into international school leaders to conclude that they are not culturally diverse; rather, she argues, they are predominantly Western, Anglophone, and male. Sanderson and Whitehead (2016) study female teachers in international schools in South Korea. They argue that there are a number of barriers to women's progression to leadership positions, including cultural beliefs about gendered roles, work-life balance in the school, self-confidence and the nature of the school hierarchy. Gardner-McTaggart (2018a) examines the characteristics of leaders of IB schools and finds that they are predominantly white, 'English' (UK or US) and Christian. Gardner-McTaggart argues that this background means that they construct leadership and international-mindedness with the mindset of their own cultural background:

> Ultimately, what international (IB) schools do, is to provide access to Englishness, under the mantle of (Anglo-European) internationalism. The policy of such schools is defined by the director. The director is chosen by the school board representing the community. The 'winning' template for IB international schools director is simple: white, English native-speaker and middle class. This generalisation works here, and what can be added with a few exceptions would be: Christian, and (predominantly) male.
>
> (Gardner-McTaggart, 2018: 113)

Correspondingly little is known about the experience of being an international school leader. The little evidence that exists suggests that it may be fraught. Benson (2011) calculates that the average tenure of an international school principal is merely 3.7 years. Reasons for departure are primarily issues with school boards, such as micromanagement, followed by career considerations. A number of studies have sought to capture the aspects of leadership that are specific to leading an international school.

In research with my colleague Mark Gibson, we have identified six key challenges faced by international school leaders – loneliness, transience, cultural differences, governance, business elements and managing school composition (Bailey & Gibson, 2019). First, international school leaders are detached from local communities so their head teachers may not have other principals to whom they can turn for advice; hence, they may feel lacking in social support for their decision-making. Second, the transience of both teachers and students may make it hard for principals to make sustained changes within their school communities. Third, the cultural diversity of international schools may lead to misunderstandings. Fourth, in many settings the governance of international schools is not regulated, and the division of responsibilities between principal and owner/school board may be indeterminate. Fifth, with the rise of for-profit schools, commercial and competitive elements of the role, for which they may feel ill-prepared, are coming to predominate. Sixth, managing the composition of both the staffing and student bodies in respect of cultural or other differences is seen as a major leadership responsibility. We argue that each of these six areas of responsibility differs markedly from the challenges faced by head teachers of government schools (Bailey & Gibson, 2019).

In line with our theme of transience as a major challenge, Murakami-Ramalho and Benham (2010) argue that dealing with the consequences of turnover is one of the major leadership challenges in international schools. They use the analogy of a fishing net to describe how everyone needs to pull together for effective change. By contrast, their case study school had been traumatized by the unexplained sacking of the previous principal, whose wife was a teacher and whose child attended the school – an intertwining of relationships that is not uncommon in international school communities – shortly before their fieldwork. Echoing our theme of the importance of business elements (Bailey & Gibson, 2019), MacDonald (2009) draws on the theory that leaders of corporations have to keep their eye on three bottom lines – the fiscal, the social and the environmental. He suggests that are equally three bottom lines for leaders of international schools – the fiscal, the academic and the 'intangible core', the last category including such things as the development of international-mindedness and student well-being.

However, other researchers have drawn attention to additional challenges that international school leaders may face. Fertig and James (2016) argue that leaders of international schools have to secure 'the institutional legitimacy of their institutions both as schools and as *international schools*' (Fertig & James, 2016: 106). Lack of clarity about an international school's constituency and stakeholders, as well as conflicting and possibly unclear regulatory frameworks, can make the process of legitimization challenging. Fertig and James (2016) see international schools – like all schools – as complex, evolving, loosely linked systems (CELLS); however, the rapid growth and rapid turnover of some international schools mean that development of connectivity, interdependence and self-organization within the institution is disrupted, rendering them particularly prone to disequilibrium between their constituent parts. In consequence, the task of leadership and management in international schools is both of greater import and less well-defined than is leadership and management of government schools.

Lee, Hallinger and Walker (2012) focus on the challenges leaders face in implementing IB programmes in schools in the Asia-Pacific region. They suggest that these challenges arise from both environmental (factors external to the organization of the school) and organization factors. This is such a loose framework as to render their work essentially descriptive rather than conceptual; nevertheless, some important findings emerge. First and foremost is the importance of context – which may be thought to render international school leadership immune to generalization. Second, they stress the intertwined nature of some of these external and internal factors. Third, they describe specific sources of challenge to leadership in the schools they study – parents and community; external assessment; private, self-funded status; organizational structures; human resource management; and curriculum, teaching and learning.

Caffyn (2018) uses the metaphor of the vampire to describe the forces, both internal and external, that suck the positive energy out of international schools. Just as the vampire threatens behavioural norms and challenges boundaries, so the international school faces contestable norms and boundaries. Teacher culture shock, turnover and subsequent transitions, tensions between local legislation and expatriate expectations, and knocks to reputation can all threaten to drain the energy of schools. Caffyn explores how this draining can be controlled or channelled by school leaders either to prevent negativity or to promote positive development.

What we see across all of these different accounts is an attempt to understand how school leaders reconcile competing demands and expectations. One recurrent theme in these studies is an emphasis on financial aspects of leading an international school – sometimes linked to specific forms of governance. A second recurrent theme is how local pressures (e.g. local regulations, expectations of the parent community) may be at odds with international expectations (e.g. assessment criteria, the wish to be seen as 'international', expectations of the non-local teaching community) – in other words, how an institution can be led in a glocalized manner. I will discuss each of these themes in the following two sections.

New Forms of Governance

Chapter 1 discussed the changing forms of governance of international schools. These changes included the expansion of for-profit education, as well as offshore campuses of prestigious Western schools, such as Branksome Hall, an elite girls' school from Toronto that has opened a campus in South Korea. Here, I consider the implications of these shifts in governance for the micropolitics of the school.

Some researchers have argued that the rise of for-profit international schooling is fundamentally shifting its purpose. For example, Kim (2019) has undertaken a systematic study of transnational education corporations. Kim argues that these corporations are having a significant impact on public education systems in Asia but these Western-based corporations are avoiding scrutiny in their home countries both because they serve elites and because their impact is elsewhere. Kim identifies four major changes involved in the rise of transnational education corporations:

1. Erosion of state regulatory powers over education. With increasing numbers of international schools, serving growing sectors of the local population, the ability of the state to decide the education of its own citizens is diminished.
2. The financialization of education. With schools seen as side-businesses in a diverse investment – perhaps as one aspect of property development, for example – they become valued for their investment value rather than their processes/product.
3. Internationalization of schooling becomes corporatization of schooling. When chains claim to be international because you are joining a global network of schools, the meaning of internationalization has changed. Global citizenship may be equated with preparation for a mobile, corporate career and replace more democratic notions of citizenship.
4. A consumer culture in education. The school becomes valued for its campus, resources and university alumni rather than for its philosophy and ethos.

In other words, Kim suggests that the rise of the for-profit motive fundamentally changes the view of the school's purpose. I suggest that, in consequence, stakeholders within the school may hold competing views which need to be balanced to maintain the organization.

Similarly, Waterson (2016) suggests that there is growing acceptance of a neoliberal market-based orthodoxy in international schools. Noting that for-profit international schools were rare at the end of the twentieth century but now constitute over two-thirds of the market, Waterson explores what this will mean for how such schools conceptualize their educational mission. He notes that whilst international schools have historically been testing grounds for new curricula and forms of pedagogy, it is unclear whether they will continue to have that role as the interests of transnational corporations come to dominate. Waterson predicts that in the profit-driven schools of the future only approaches that generate income or improve measurable results will be targeted; however, further research is needed to confirm or deny this hypothesis.

Kim (2019) and Waterson (2016) raise important concerns, but data collected from within international schools suggests that the emerging situation is more complex. In James and Sheppard's (2014) study, principals felt that governors tried to micromanage regardless of whether the school was for-profit or not-for-profit. In addition, James and Sheppard argue that in practice the for-profit/not-for-profit distinction lacks clarity; the status of a school can change over time, and owners can benefit in various ways even in an ostensibly not-for-profit institution. Their participants who led for-profit schools felt that they were nevertheless able to maintain their educational mission. James and Sheppard point out that accrediting organizations currently do not monitor changes in governance, and suggest that schools should be required to report any such changes since secure governance – of whichever model – should be a central concern of accreditation.

Machin (2014) argues that principals in for-profit schools have to be comfortable with discourses of education that are simultaneously educational and commercial. Based on interviews with fifteen principals of for-profit schools in China, Malaysia and Thailand, Machin identifies ways in which commercial discourses permeated the interviews (for example, one principals referred to parents as 'clients'), and the tensions that some principals expressed between these two ways of framing their school's purpose (for example, pressure to admit students regardless of whether their educational needs could be met). Machin identifies one particular tension being that many owners micromanaged their schools, encroaching into what the principals saw as their role. In many schools, the appointment of a school business manager aimed to enable the principals to focus on educational issues, but some principals reported that the Business Manager encroached on aspects of their role and undermined their authority. Machin argues that longer-established principals in the study were more comfortable with the educational role, whereas newer principals were adopting a hybridized commercial-educational discourse.

Balancing the Global with the Local

Throughout these accounts, then, is a common theme of competing visions for the organizational culture of international schools, with school principals warily navigating these micropolitics. One recurrent tension that these leaders report is having to manage the tensions between global and local considerations for their schools. This echoes wider scholarship on educational leadership, such as Walker and Quong's (1998) suggestion that in a global society leaders of all schools increasingly need to balance conformity and diversity in their communities. Keller (2015) argues that leadership of international schools involves the management of dualities, invoking the image of the Roman god Janus, who simultaneously looks in two opposite directions, to capture what international school leaders need to do. The dualities that Keller mentions are both spatial (between different geographically rooted cultures) and temporal (between forward-looking and traditional forms of education). In my research into international school principals with Mark Gibson, however, it was clear that many international school principals conflated the two, with the local being seen as backward-looking and the global being seen as the future. In this section, I look at two arenas in which these tensions between the global and the local must be navigated by school leaders.

School composition

School composition is a reflection of two issues – the composition of the teaching body (through recruitment, remuneration and retention), and the composition of the study body (a result of student admissions). I discuss both these issues in this section.

Research has suggested that high levels of teacher turnover are a feature of many international schools. Turnover in international schools sometimes extends to the leaders themselves as well as presenting a problem for leadership (Bunnell, 2019). For example, Mancuso, Roberts and White (2010) surveyed teacher retention in schools in the Near East South Asia Council of Overseas Schools (an organization for American international schools) and found an average annual turnover rate of 17 per cent, ranging from no turnover in some schools to as high as 60 per cent in others. Factors influencing turnover were varied, and included both personal characteristics and organizational conditions. Personal characteristics that impacted on turnover included marriage and age; teachers who were married to another teacher were more likely to be planning to move than those with a non-teaching spouse; and, surprisingly, middle-aged teachers were more likely to be planning a move than their older or younger colleagues. Organizational conditions impacting on turnover included perceptions of leadership, faculty influence in decision-making and satisfaction with level of salary. Leadership and turnover are intrinsically connected, with unsupportive leadership often cited as a reason for high turnover (Mancuso, Roberts & White, 2010) but leadership style was also a consequence of high turnover rates, as leaders then needed to focus their energy on rebuilding community ethos year after year.

In 2018, the Council of British International Schools commissioned a study into teacher supply to international schools, which looked at both recruitment and retention from the perspectives of teachers and school leaders. The fact that they commissioned this extensive study reflects a concern that, as international schooling expands rapidly, schools will be unable to find sufficient teachers to meet their increasing needs (COBIS, 2018). The report was also eager to ensure that international schools are not seen as a drain on teacher supply within the UK; COBIS stressed that many teachers recruited to international schools were otherwise thinking of leaving the profession, and that international school experience often led teachers to return back home feeling energized and upskilled.

Bunnell (2019) identifies what he terms the 'Growth Paradox' of international schooling, whereby the research suggests this is a sector in which there is insecurity and precarity, yet teachers and leaders continue to be recruited to international schools. This is possibly explained by the fact that turnover is often viewed negatively in the literature (for example, Mancuso, Roberts and White's (2010) discussion implies that principals will want to reduce turnover), whereas teachers and leaders themselves sometimes welcome this fluidity in employment, as it enables both the organization and individuals to grow and change, and they enjoy being taken out of their comfort zones (Bailey, 2015b; Bunnell, 2019).

What is not stressed in the literature, however, is that turnover is a consequence of the pull that international schools experience between the local and the global. The decision to recruit 'global' teachers necessarily implies teachers who feel a pull to other places – to return home or progress to other countries. Some international schools recruit host-country educators who become the ballast giving stability to the staffroom, whereas others insist that only educators from an Anglophone country need apply.

In addition to management of the composition of the staffroom, studies suggest that international school leaders actively manage the composition of their student body (Bailey & Gibson, 2019), seeking to prevent dominance by any single ethnicity or nationality. In the study I conducted with Mark Gibson, principals expressed concerns about a number of issues related to the composition of the student body; for example, if one single nationality comes to predominate, the school will no longer be seen as truly 'international', and that other parents will worry that their children will be linguistically or culturally excluded by the dominant group. Balancing local market conditions with the wish to be seen as global is therefore a central concern of many international school principals.

Teacher turnover and student composition are intrinsically linked to the issue of ethos that we turn to next.

School ethos

Noting that most recent expansion in international schooling has occurred in the Asia Pacific region and the developing world, Gardener-McTaggart (2018b) uses two concepts to capture the ethos of an international school, that of the 'imperial gaze' and the idea of 'cultural laundering'. The idea of the imperial gaze is an adaptation of the 'male gaze' developed in feminist theory, where a female feels she must react as if she is being scrutinized by a male. Similarly, it can be suggested, the students of international schools learn to behave as if being watched by a Western eye, an eye that values an Ivy League (or at least Western) university education, 'Englishness', Western forms of dress and so on. The concept of cultural laundering is based on an analogy with financial laundering whereby the origins of assets are concealed through international transactions and the money thereby rendered seemingly 'clean'; similarly, cultural practices may be appropriated through the process of international schooling to prepare, say, Asian students for university life in a Western university. Both of these concepts offer insights, but also have limitations; I would argue that the concept of cultural laundering has the merit of affording more agency to the students than is given in the concept of the imperial gaze, but at the cost of implying that their accrual of a Western education is somehow illicit.

Empirical studies suggest that the ethos of international schools can be dominated by Western values. For example, Gardner-McTaggart's (2019a) study of directors of IB schools, albeit based on a small sample, suggests that many are explicitly committed to Anglo-Christian values and see their role as 'giving back' to the world (despite the many material and other benefits that the position accrues). In addition, he charts how Western humanism permeates the IB framework, particularly its form of commitment to Global Citizenship Education. A further example is found in Hammad and Shah's (2018) study of leadership of international schools in Saudi Arabia. They identify areas of tension between the liberal approach that predominates in international schools and the conservative context of Saudi Arabia. Their interviews with school leaders show how culturally sensitive areas such as Saudization (of the workforce), sex segregation and parental expectations are managed. The leaders explain their two strategies of either compliance or circumvention. The tension between the local and the global, and how both are entwined in the schools' ethos, is clearly demonstrated through this study.

Another aspect of school ethos is the leadership style, which then permeates relationships between members of staff. In the growing body of research into leadership styles in international schools, several studies have suggested that instructional leadership is the dominant style (Javadi, Bush & Ng, 2017; Velarde, 2017), whilst others have pointed to the use of distributed leadership in some international schools (Bunnell, 2008a; Hallinger & Lee, 2012). Hallinger and Lee (2012) find that distributed instructional leadership is the predominant form of leadership in IB schools, suggesting that the programmes and ethos of the IB may be encouraging distributed practices. What these studies have in common is that Western theories of leadership seem to 'fit' international schools. Again, then, we can see a tension between the global and the local being played out through the micropolitics of international schools.

Three Examples

Example 1: Leading a for-profit, chain school in Malaysia

George *[a pseudonym]* is the principal of an international school operated by a chain based in Malaysia, although he had only been in post for a few months at the time of the interview. This was his fourth principalship of an international school; before that, he had been a school principal in his home country. All of his international schools have been for-profit schools, and George said that coming into such an environment had been a major adjustment:

> They have all been for-profit schools. So it's been an adjustment to the mentality of such an organization. Not that I'm uncomfortable with it at all because at the root of it all is the welfare and the education that we are providing a good for young people and I think that remains as the most important aspect of my work anyway.

George stressed that for-profit schools differed widely in the role that they gave to the principal:

> Where some want you to be at the grassroots level in the classrooms and others want you to be fulfilling more of the CEO type, more remote just simply by the pressure of paperwork and planning and strategy and all those sorts of things.

His work is overseen by the management of the chain corporation. He saw advantages to working for a chain organization; for example, when need arises, central administration staff can be seconded to work in the school for a period. In addition, others in the organization can offer the principal a useful sounding board from outside their school. At the time of the interview, he was satisfied that there was a clear demarcation of responsibilities between the central corporation and his own role, and that he had operational autonomy:

> I've been in other schools where they've got the corporates involved in the education side of it, and you know they are not good bed fellows, really. There is a lack of understanding and appreciation. The two don't marry perfectly at all.

George explained that the recession in the oil industry was changing the composition of the student body, with a reduced number of expatriates and increased numbers of Malaysians. He was working with the admissions department to ensure that the school didn't end up being 'dominated' by a single nationality. George talked at length about the cultural conflicts that can arise between different stakeholders in an international school. He explained an incident that had happened in one of his previous schools where the expectations of teachers and expectations of parents from a different culture came into conflict:

> A staff member asked a child to pick up a piece of paper that they had dropped on the cafeteria floor, and then [we were] called to account by the French parents who had issued a formal letter of complaint to the police, who then had to come to the school to file a report about this sort of brutality to children. Coming from Dubai, where it's basically a nanny mentality, and everyone had probably two or three of them anyway, and understanding that this is just the modus operandi of some people.

He felt that part of this came from the sense of entitlement that some parents have in international school; George observed 'Just because you pay fees, it doesn't necessarily entitle you to behave like a fruit loop.' However, he also acknowledged that there were differences in the backgrounds of different stakeholders that made clear communication a particularly important part of international school leadership. For instance, he discussed the Chinese Malaysian parents at his current school:

The Chinese [Malaysians] have been brought up in an education system that is very traditional, very demanding and very focused, and that's not the way we do things in teaching and learning anymore. There are other ways to skin the cat where the kids can actually enjoy the process of learning. And so it's being proactive in getting the parents in and explaining the sorts of strategies that schools employ nowadays, and how important is the partnership of the parents with the school and their child in arriving at the best outcomes, and so on and so forth. So that's all been all a new learning curve over the course of the decade or so I've been away.

In conclusion, George emphasized the importance of an international school principal facing difficulties with flexibility and a strong sense of humour:

I think you just have to have the preparedness to roll with things because not everything rolls out the way you would normally expect it to roll out. Because each country is uniquely different in the way they do things.

Example 2: Leading a predominantly expatriate, non-profit school in China

Ken *[a pseudonym]* is the principal of an IB school serving mainly expatriate families in China who participated in an IB-funded research into well-being in their schools (Cooker, Bailey, Stevenson & Joseph, 2016). When the research team visited his school, he had been the principal for five years. Prior to that he had worked in other leadership positions in the same school and at another school in the Middle East.

Ken had experienced many challenges that were specific to leading an international school in China. For example, one of the major issues for the school is air quality. He explained that there are air purification machines in every classroom, and daily checks of air quality in the school. Every year, the school brings in an air pollutant consultant, and they are continually updating the equipment that they use. In addition, he mentioned the importance of making sure that the Communist Party were satisfied with decisions (there is a Party representative within every school).

However, his main challenges were the expatriate nature of his school, with the problems that it brings for students and the distance that the school has from the local Chinese community. There is a high level of turnover of both staff and students ('about 25% of people are different every year'). He said that whilst the school tries not to be a foreign outcrop, this kind of turnover makes it a challenge as it takes people a While to feel comfortable reaching out to the Chinese community. He was also concerned about health and safety issues when involving students in work with the Chinese community:

> There are more difficulties with roads, and there are more difficulties with people touching anybody with blonde hair, and so there are limits to what we can do within the duty of care.

Despite these reservations, the school runs a number of programmes for the local community, ranging from English language tuition to a community dance programme.

A second major challenge was the impact of the parental lifestyles on the children. Firstly, the majority of students are Third Culture Kids – being raised in a country outside their parents' cultures – and the school is conscious of the potential sense of dislocation that this may bring. Consequently, the school works hard at creating a sense of belonging for them, despite their mobile lifestyles. Secondly, because of the privileged demographic of these mobile families, many students are essentially being raised by their maids, with parents having little direct involvement. Ken claimed:

> Sometimes the only time the parents interface with the children is when we get a problem.

As a result, the school places a lot of emphasis on offering pastoral support to students; Ken emphasized that this was not something that was left to the school counsellor, but is seen as the responsibility of every adult in the school. For example, during our visit he was highly visible around the school and spent time interacting directly with students.

Ken works hard to create a warm and supportive environment in the school, but the continual turnover means that he has to re-establish this every academic year as 'there would be a good number of new people and sometimes they come in and they change the dynamic'.

Example 3: Leading a predominantly Emirati school owned by an Emirati family in the UAE

James *[a pseudonym]* is the principal of an IB school in the UAE in which the majority of students are Emirati. The research team visited him as part of an IB-funded project to examine their Middle Years Programme (Stevenson et al., 2017). James had been principal of the school for just over a year at the time of the interview; prior to that, he had led a number of schools in his home country. James was the fourth principal the school had had in the last eight years.

He expressed frustration with working in the UAE, largely around finance, bureaucracy and how decisions were communicated to the school:

> From a cultural perspective, coming out of this part of the world with the rapid growth over the last twenty to thirty years in this country, maybe the education system has put in some control mechanisms that were initially set out to support schools but I think now are actually constricting and prohibiting school development and decision-making The KHDA mandates what you can and can't do in terms of the financing, and if you are unfortunately an unsuccessful school or unsatisfactory in their eyes, *[you are stopped from raising school fees and]* you have got nowhere to go in terms of raising funds to change things ... Secondly I think that the constricting nature everything seems to be highly bureaucratic and paper based, from registration and parent and school contracts to re-registration year in and year out. As a young country from an education perspective and not having that universal view and teacher standards and that type of thing, they have just not got in place at the moment so there are a few areas of difference ... As I am the principal of the school, *[the local authorities]* have our contact details and yet we seem to understand school and education policy via newspapers. There is no communication to say, well, this is the policy and there is no opportunity to discuss that with the school.

He also discussed cultural differences between the school and the Emirati parents around how education is conceptualized, with homework seen as encroaching on family time, which is central to Emirati culture:

> Our Emirati families may not see the value or the role of outside school learning in terms of the time outside of school where the students would be working. Some of our families would see that as being quite inhibiting and disruptive to family life.

He explained that the school translates all of its communication with parents into Arabic, but that far more than that was needed to reach a shared understanding with parents:

> When I am working with parents it is ... trying to get that conversation across because it is not so much the translation; it is the translation of the meaning and intent.

He explained some of the challenges he had in working with staff, wanting to build their capacity, but also recognizing that they were struggling with constant changes in school leadership. He had found it hard to recruit quality staff to a relatively new school. Overall, he described his job as 'like flying the airplane as you are building the wings'.

Conceptualizing Leadership and Hierarchy

This micropolitics occurs with a background of contested views of leadership, hierarchy and decision-making within international schools. There is a growing body of evidence that suggests that views of effective leadership and organizations differ across cultures (Hofstede, 2001). Whilst there are some characteristics of effective leadership that seem to be universal (for example, inspiring others), other dimensions of leadership vary between countries (Scandura & Dorfman, 2004). For example, degrees of power distance, individualist versus collective approaches to decision-making, extent of uncertainty avoidance, the value placed on traditionally masculine or feminine traits and a short-term versus a long-term orientation have been shown empirically to be clustered in specific societies (Hofstede, 2001). In a study of Swiss military officers, Rockstuhl et al. (2011) show that cross-cultural intelligence is a stronger predictor of leadership effectiveness than either general intelligence or emotional intelligence, for those leaders who had cross-border leadership responsibilities, whereas for leaders with only domestic responsibilities, emotional intelligence was a stronger predictor. For the past twenty years, educational theorists have started to explore the importance of cultural contexts on educational leadership, and caution against wholesale adoption of Western theories (Hallinger & Leithwood, 1998).

For the leader of an international school, who may have stakeholders from a range of different countries each with their own cultural expectations of good leadership, this can present a challenge. I have explored how aspects of school leadership may differ between Western and Gulf Cooperation Council countries with colleagues from the Bahrain Teachers College (Bailey et al., 2021), identifying four key differences – what is school leadership, who becomes a school leader, how leaders are best supported and whether leaders believe they can succeed. Specific characteristics of good leadership that are valued in many Arab societies are being humble, familial and religious. In our article, we note that there is more emphasis in GCC cultures on positional rather than personal leadership. In addition, power distance may make it hard for leadership supports widely used in Western society, such as coaching and mentoring, to be effective. Finally, the Islamic concept of *shura*, whereby leaders gather views and concerns from a wide sector of society and seek consensus, may come into conflict with Western views of incisive decision-making. In consequence, a school leader in the Middle East may find it hard to behave in such a way that both Western and Arab teachers, students and parents see them as an effective leader.

Leadership is a relational concept (leadership requires followers), which implies that understanding leadership involves understanding the community which that individual leads. In consequence, there is an emerging literature that employs social identity theory (Tajfel, 1972; Tajfel & Turner, 1979) to understand effective leadership of organizations. Social identity theory argues that the question 'Who am I?' can be answered in multiple ways by any individual, along a continuum from personal characteristics to 'the groups to which I belong'. According to this theory, self-categorization into groups underpins many behaviours, especially those that are oriented towards group (rather than individual) interests. In particular, much of the literature in this field suggests that prototypicality is a feature of effective leadership. Put simply, effective leaders are seen embodying a prototype, i.e. as possessing the multidimensional attributes of in-group membership – the key features that differentiate it from other groups. Moreover, since we all have multiple social identities, in work organizations the employer will seek to make organizational identity salient to its employees. Although much of the empirical work in this area has been on emergent leadership (Hogg, 2001), the positional leadership of, say, school principals can also be viewed through this lens.

In a diverse organization, such as an international school, making the collective identity salient to members may be particularly challenging. Moreover, prototypicality of leadership may be either impossible or impractical when a diverse staff is involved. Steffens et al. (2014) have argued that the emphasis on prototypicality needs to be complemented by analysis of other ways in which the leader may manage group identity management; in particular, they proffer a view of leadership as the ability of leaders to create, represent, reinforce and promote the sense of group membership (Steffens et al., 2014). Essentially, in a diverse organization, the prototype may need to be negotiated and agreed (Al Muqarshi, Kaparou & Kelly, 2020); cultural diversity may undermine effective organizational leadership unless 'identity entrepreneurship' (Steffens et al., 2014) is pursued, that is an active crafting of what it means to be 'one of us'.

Despite these theoretical insights, there is a paucity of empirical research exploring their implications for leadership practices in international schools. Calnin et al. (2018) describe the leadership intelligences identified by the IB, but include no data from school leaders themselves. A few studies have drawn on leadership theories in analysing international schools, drawing attention to the dominance of instructional leadership in IB schools (e.g. Javadi, Bush & Ng, 2017). The limited number of studies that explore how the leaders manage micropolitics of cultural diversity are examined in the following section.

Leading Diverse School Communities

Two studies have highlighted the conflicts that may erupt as a consequence of leading international schools. In both cases, the researchers draw attention to the tensions that can result from having a transient (usually international) leadership and teaching staff working alongside a more permanent (often local) staff, with each group feeling that they embody the 'true' spirit of the school.

Barakat and Brooks (2016) examine an American international school in Egypt to understand how culture impacts on leadership. They argue that different cultural expectations about leadership and instructional styles create tensions for school leaders in such a context. For example, whereas American culture values competition and results, Egyptian culture values collaborative processes. Moreover, social values may result in different beliefs about the remit of a school. They offer the example of an extracurricular programme in which American and Egyptian staff disagreed over whether the school should teach abstinence in sex education, with the American principal and American teachers largely disagreeing with the Egyptian owner and Egyptian teachers.

Bunnell (2018) does not look at the micropolitics from the leaders' perspective; rather, he examines teachers' social media comments concerning international school principals, charting the personal diatribes on named individuals that were posted on one particular site devoted to international schooling. Bunnell points out that there is frequently no pressure valve in international schools that disgruntled staff can use to express their feelings. Bunnell's conclusion from the comments is that international school teachers are working in a situation of precarity (which I discuss further in Chapter 4), although few of the comments chart actual working conditions. He argues: 'Many of the comments on ISR.com are undeniably damning and deep-felt accusations, coming as they do from professional educators' (Bunnell, 2018: 561). Bunnell points a potential finger of blame at 'Penelopes' – long-standing members of staff who are loyal to the country where they reside – whom he stereotypes as follows: 'This character is easily identified in any staffroom – they were once useful and hardworking but now sit out their time doing the regular things' (Bunnell, 2018: 562). Despite this questionable analysis, his paper usefully highlights the kinds of pressures that are faced by international school leaders in the age of the internet, and the tensions that can exist within diverse staffing bodies.

Conclusion

This chapter has focused on the micropolitics of international schools, largely from the perspective of school principals, focusing on the impact of the blurred and complex cultural context in which many international school principals operate and the tensions they may feel as a result. My colleague Mark Gibson and I suggest that the defensive manner in which principals defend working for a for-profit school may be a result of affective dissonance (Gibson & Bailey, forthcoming), whereby they feel a disconnect between their personal values and the puppet-master of market realities. Before finishing this chapter, it is worth highlighting that international schools are simply experiencing in condensed or highlighted form some of the organizational changes that are beginning in public systems of education worldwide. School leaders in many contexts are now leading culturally diverse organizations, and commercial pressures on educational leaders are increasing as a result of quasi-markets for education in the public sector. The international school sector offers insight into some of the dangers and the opportunities for the leadership of schooling in evolving systems of education. International schools are one site in which the results of the marketization of education and the globalization of educational institutions can be examined and may alert us to possible further change in wider systems of education.

Of course, the perspective of school leaders must necessarily be complemented by the perspectives of other stakeholders in international schooling. In Chapters 4–6, we explore specific aspects of the institutions that these principals are leading. First, we look at the staffroom and then we look inside the classroom, by considering international school teachers in Chapter 4 and their learners and curriculum in Chapters 5 and 6.

4

Teaching in International Schools

Introduction

It is estimated that there could be as many as 800,000 international school teachers by the year 2026 (Bunnell, 2017). To put that in perspective, that is nearly double the number of teachers in England. Yet there is surprisingly little research into this group of teachers. In this chapter, it is argued that study of international school teachers merits further attention – their motivations for leaving public systems of schooling, their view of their professional identity and their work – both as worthy as study in its own right and as offering insights into the public systems of education that they leave (and to which they may choose to return). Study of international school teachers provides insights into the impact of neoliberal globalization on the identities and class positioning of globally mobile professionals.

This chapter examines the burgeoning literature on international school teachers in order to understand both the nature of the role and their professional identities. We introduce a range of theoretical lenses that have been proposed for understanding international school teaching – Third Culture Teachers and accidental teachers (Bailey & Cooker, 2019) – as well as discussion about the class position and precarity of international school teachers' work (Rey, Bolay & Gez, 2020). This chapter builds on such work by examining the extent to which international school teachers develop a shared identity that enables them collectively to shape the future of their schools, or whether the transient nature of international school teaching and Balkanized nature of international school staffrooms renders their practices and identities essentially reactive to the market pressures of neoliberal globalization. It is argued that although the growth of international schools is one of a palette of changes to schooling globally that could serve to intensify and de-professionalize teachers' work (Bailey, 2000; Bailey, 2015b), the available data suggest that working in international schools can paradoxically re-professionalize and re-empower teachers. I suggest that some international school teachers are part of the Global Middle Class, although other theorists have posited that they are part of the global precariat (Bunnell, 2016; Poole, 2019a). In other words, globalization is simultaneously both risky and empowering for international school teachers.

Teachers in International Schools

We know a little about who becomes an international school teacher. Traditionally, most were British or American in origin, but in recent years other Western countries have been the source of increasing numbers of these teachers (Resnik, 2017). Bunnell (2017) points out that we know a few stark statistics about the demographics within these national groupings, such as that 72 per cent are under the age of 40 and 48 per cent are single.

Researchers have speculated about ways in which the source of international school teachers may change over coming years, as the global market for international school teachers develops. For example, Bunnell (2014) argues that international schools may be currently draining teachers from the state sector in the UK and other developed countries, whilst noting that in future this drain of qualified teachers may come from poorer parts of the world. On the other hand, data suggest that these countries will continue to be a rich source of teachers; as many as 46 per cent of British teachers have an interest in working overseas (Morgan, Sives & Appleton, 2006). International school recruiters seek a number of characteristics in addition to general teaching capabilities – adaptability to being in a foreign setting, cultural sensitivity and pedagogical flexibility, as well as being a right 'fit' for a particular school (Budrow & Tarc, 2018). The future sources of international school teachers will in part be a reflection of how well teacher education programmes in different settings develop such characteristics.

International school teachers cannot be seen as a homogeneous grouping, but several researchers have sought to identify shared characteristics, often distinguished by subgroups. Back in 2001, Hardman categorized international school teachers applying from overseas into three groups: childless career professionals, mavericks (free and independent spirits) or career professionals with families. In addition, he categorized older teachers without dependent children into three more groups: senior career professionals, senior mavericks and senior 'Penelopes' (who are loyal to their adopted country, the name comes from Ulysses's wife in *The Odyssey*). Since the time of Hardman's (2001) work, there has been a growth in the number of host-country nationals working in international schools, and some theorists have noted that the expansion of schools has led to a diversity in the types of educators being sought. For example, Poole (2020a) studies what he terms 'Chinese internationalized schools', that is, a school following both an international and a Chinese curriculum, so that it offers bilingual education. He argues that whereas teachers in traditional international schools tend to be Anglophone, qualified teachers, the teachers working in the schools he studies are often either Anglophone but lacking teacher qualifications, or non-Anglophone.

Much of the work done in this area has been focused on helping recruiters to identify the demographic origins and motivations of people most likely to be recruited and retained as international school teachers. Whilst this information provides some insight into who chooses to become an international school educator, the focus in this chapter is rather than on the experience itself and other consequences of that choice. Although theories of globalization may suggest that the ideal global worker fits seamlessly into workplaces around the world, by contrast empirical study suggests a messiness to transitions in the global market for international school teachers. I will suggest that this messiness is not necessarily experienced as a negative thing.

Teachers' Work in International Schools

There is a growing number of studies that illuminate the many ways in which working in an international school is very different to working in other kinds of schools (Halicioglu, 2015).

We see in this section that many teachers view their work in international schools as having a number of advantages over working in their home country – amongst the pulls mentioned are higher salaries, opportunities to get broader experiences, travel possibilities, less stressful working conditions and the ability to choose a curriculum that accords with an individual's educational ideals.

Equally, the work involves a number of challenges. First, culture shock – both in the country at large and specifically in the work setting – may impact negatively on teachers. The professional culture shock experienced by some teachers on joining international schools is illustrated by a small-scale study at a British school in an unnamed country in SE Asia, during which seven out of the twelve participants broke their contracts and left the school (Roskell, 2013). All of these teachers explained that whilst they had expected culture shock in adjusting to living in a new country, they had not anticipated a workplace culture shock, and were shocked by some of the procedures at their new school. Resnik (2017) notes that international school teachers may feel challenged by the gender and other cultural norms of the countries where they work; she notes the tension they may experience in their professional lives between passing on their own values and reinforcing those of the host culture. Savva (2013) studies North American teacher experiences in international schools, suggesting that the struggles they experience with being in a foreign country often lead them to a deep intercultural understanding. Savva argues that some, but not all, teachers use this enhanced understanding to improve their professional practice.

Second, there may be additional workload consequent upon the particular challenges in international schools. Sunder (2013) uses Hoschchild's work on emotional labour to suggest that teachers in international schools have a particularly large workload in this respect. Whilst all teachers have to do this, the need to be sensitive to cultural context and the constant transitions in international schools create additional demands on international school teachers. In an article focusing on public relations practitioners, Bunnell (2006) discusses the multiple factors leading to role stress within international schools – for PRPs, leaders and teachers alike. In particular, he stresses the high turnover of stakeholders – teachers, students, administrators and trustees alike – which Bunnell argues can sometimes be 'debilitating' (Bunnell, 2006: 388).

It is important to recognize that there may be considerable divergence even within an institution as to how teachers perceive their work. Poole (2018) charts differences between how Chinese teachers and expatriate teachers viewed the school's organizational identity at a Type C international school (Hayden & Thompson, 2013) in China. The Chinese teachers were more likely to describe it as a Chinese school and to explain school practices in terms of Chinese culture, whereas expatriate teachers were more likely to describe school practices in terms of its commitment to being international. From Poole's study, we can see that there can be marked differences in how teachers conceptualize their work within the same international school.

Teacher Identity in International Schools

The different work involved in being an educator in an international school can impact on teachers' professional identity. For some teachers, this has meant a developed sense of being part of a global world of teachers; for others, it has meant falling into teaching in a way that they would be unable to do in their own country. In this section, I shall consider three conceptual lenses I have developed with my colleague Lucy Cooker (Bailey & Cooker, 2019) for understanding international school teachers' professional identity. Whilst there is insufficient space to delve into the complex conceptualization of teacher identity here (Edwards & Edwards, 2017), it is worth noting that it is multidimensional and not amenable to simple analysis. These lenses are therefore not competing theoretical accounts, but can be drawn on like tools from a toolbox in order to understand specific groups of teachers in specific countries or types of school. A single teacher may also change how they see themselves in different situations or over time. Before examining these lenses, I begin by noting that there seem to be key distinctions between how host-country and expatriate teachers believe their role is seen within international schools.

In my article examining the professional identity of expatriate teachers in an international school in Malaysia (Bailey, 2015b), I argue that whilst the teachers experienced challenges and a sense of insecurity, they felt energized rather than threatened by them. They reported that their work was less intensive and stressful than in their home countries; I noted the irony that in a private international school they felt fewer market pressures than they had in the public education systems where they had previously worked. The participants in my research had initially felt deskilled upon arriving in a very different cultural and institutional setting, but in the longer term felt that their skills had been improved by the experience. On the other hand, I argued, their host-country teaching colleagues were deskilled by a discourse in which their teaching strategies were viewed as inferior to those of the expatriate educators.

A similar unease with the differentials between host-country and expatriate teachers is seen in the work of Fimyar (2018), who interviewed eleven expatriate teachers at three international schools in Kazakhstan in order to explore their identity. She notes that expatriate and local teachers were given separate staffrooms – ostensibly so that neither disturbed the other when interacting in their own language. In addition, there were significant differentials between international and local teachers; local teachers received lower pay and were expected to work a six-day week, whereas international recruits had higher salaries and were expected to work a five-day week. Expatriate teachers believed that they didn't only have to teach, but also had a second role – to develop local teachers and schools – that many had only learnt about after arriving in the country. Again, the assumption is that the expatriate teachers were more highly skilled than their local counterparts.

A concern with teacher agency has also featured in accounts of host-country teachers working in international schools. The participants in Lai, Li and Gong's (2016) study of Chinese language teachers at thirteen international schools in Hong Kong reflected on the pedagogical decisions they made, critically reflecting on both Western, student-centred approaches and traditional pedagogies, seeking to establish a balance between the two. It was also evident that whilst Western colleagues could influence their instructional approaches, this was a one-way relationship, with their own pedagogical skills not being recognized. In addition, the teachers seemed to occupy a marginal position in the school; the only school events in which they were given a leading role were those pertaining to Chinese culture.

This is not to say, however, that all expatriate teachers have agency and a sense of empowerment. Teachers' sense of agency seems to be closely related to the leadership style within their school (Everitt, 2020). Everitt's study of six non-Peruvian teachers working at different international schools in Lima found variability in how much power and sense of agency the teachers enjoyed, and this was closely linked to their decision to renew their contracts.

Despite these important differentials, the majority of the literature on international school teachers has implicitly focused on conceptualizing the identity of expatriate educators. This literature, then, provides an example of how professional identity may shift in relation to global mobility. I shall briefly consider three concepts that I have proposed with Lucy Cooker for making sense of international school teachers' identities.

Third Culture Teachers

A study I conducted with my colleague Lucy Cooker (Bailey & Cooker, 2019) of international school teachers enrolling on a postgraduate courses with a British university suggests that many teachers in international schools have found their professional identity and practices have been affected by their experiences of professional mobility, with both being (re)formed through their work in international schools. Adapting the work of Third Culture Kids that has been used to understand the identities of students in international schools, who no longer belong to their passport country nor to their country of residence, we argue that Third Culture Teachers identify as an international school teacher more than they do with the teaching profession in their country of residence. They feel detached from teaching in their country of origin.

This concept ties in with the work of previous researchers who have noted that working in an international school can impact upon teacher identity and professional practices. Teacher identity is not fixed, and even the identities of experienced teachers evolve to fit the institutional context of their international school (Bunnell, Fertig & James, 2020). Reflecting on her own professional journey, Joslin (2002) identifies several aspects of working in international school that impacted on her professional practice, including the culture of her current setting, her current school and of the previous institutions in which she has worked. Based on a study of teachers in IB schools, Bunnell, Fertig and James (2020) suggest that although such institutionalization could be seen as coercive, it is widely welcomed by teachers. They note that participants had a strong sense of belonging to the global IB community, and that becoming an IB teacher had involved a considerable investment of their personal time and resources in order to meet the pedagogic expectations of the organization. In other words, they had embraced their identity as IB teachers.

Accidental teachers

Poole (2020a) has pointed out that many Type C international schools are employing growing numbers of non-qualified Anglophone teachers – that is, individuals who have not pursued the traditional teacher career pathway that commences with a teaching qualification. In my paper with Lucy Cooker (Bailey & Cooker, 2019), we argue that in some international schools there are a number of 'accidental teachers' – individuals who set out to travel and experience a new culture, and who became teachers incidentally, as a way to support this lifestyle. Whilst many international schools only employ qualified teachers, there is a subgroup of schools who are happy to employ unqualified native speakers of English in their classrooms. There is now a growing market in distance qualifications offered by Western universities to unqualified teachers working in international schools, in order to assist their professional development.

A typology of international school teachers

In Chapter 1, I introduced Hayden and Thompson's (2013) typology of international schools: Type A schools are the traditional type, established to serve the children of globally mobile parents; Type B schools are the ideological type, set up to promote international-mindedness, peace and international understanding; Type C schools are the non-traditional type, established to serve the local middle class, and typically run for profit.

In my paper with Lucy Cooker (Bailey & Cooker, 2019), we argue that, similarly, international school teachers differ in their raison d'être, and propose that there are three types of expatriate international school teachers. Type A teachers have a primary commitment to mobility and travel (just as Type A schools are there to support globally mobile workers), Type B teachers have an ideological commitment to internationalism (echoing the ideological orientation of Type B schools) and Type C teachers have a primary commitment to their adopted country (just as Type C schools predominantly serve the host-country middle class). We do not assume that a particular type of school has a specific type of teacher; indeed, any type of school could be expected to have a range of different types of teachers. The purpose of our typology is to understand the diverse motivations and conceptions of their professional work and identity which international school teachers may hold. We also describe how teachers can move between these different ideal types, drawing on the biographical narratives of our research participants to illustrate this point (Bailey & Cooker, 2019). This is an area that deserves further research, as it seems that being international in their teaching has become for some teachers a technology of subjectification (Foucault, 1988). Poole (2020b) complements this approach by emphasizing a dialogic and fluid approach to teacher identity. Building upon our work (Bailey & Cooker, 2019), Poole shows how the identity of his single case study teacher, Tyron, evolves in part through the narratives constructed over the period of data collection. For Poole, Tyron is 'stranded in a borderland identity' (p. 12), and actively uses the interview encounters to assert 'multiplicitous' (p. 13) identities. Poole's work shows the rich potential of such a conceptual approach to understanding international school teacher identity but needs replication beyond his single case study.

In summary, research suggests that employment in an international school may impact upon both teachers' work and their professional identity in multiple ways, that there are significant differences between host-country and expatriate teachers in both of these respects, and that changes in the international school sector may be expected to have further impact. In the following section, I consider the effect of such changes in work, working conditions and identity on the socio-economic position of teachers in international schools.

A Global Precariat?

Some commentators have argued that international school teachers form a 'global educational precariat' (Bunnell, 2016; Poole, 2019a). 'Precariat' is a term coined by Standing (2011) to capture the employment insecurity experienced by an emergent class as a result of neoliberal economics. It was an attempt to capture sociologically the effects of labour market flexibility, but its broad, sweeping claims end up grouping together part-time workers, migrants, call-centre workers and criminals, and the diversity between these groups is at least as startling as the similarities (Spencer, 2012). Standing notes that this insecurity is often experienced by those on the margins of citizenship such as migrants and refugees. He also argues that at times the flexibility offered by being in the precariat can feel liberating. Standing's work has come in for considerable criticism, not least for its lack of empirical basis (Conley, 2012).

Despite these weaknesses, in recent years this concept has been used to analyse the position of international school teachers (Bunnell, 2016; Poole, 2019a). Bunnell (2016) analyses the online comments of disgruntled teachers on international educator chats and juxtaposes these to a handful of high-profile cases where international teachers have become embroiled in political, diplomatic or sensationalized media incidents to suggest that international school teachers can be easily sacked, deported or even arrested because they lack legal rights in their country of residence. Poole (2019a) analyses data collected from only four international school teachers in Shanghai to support the thesis of precarity, arguing that these four teachers lacked a sense of agency, felt financially insecure and believed that their professional identities were not fully affirmed; in particular, he draws attention to their lack of representation in labour disputes, to employment uncertainty and a lack of the qualifications that would enable them to seek teaching jobs back home. Both Bunnell and Poole acknowledge the limitations of their data, and argue that further research needs to be done to explore this concept in relation to international school teachers. However, it is hard to see what would constitute counter-evidence to this hypothesis. Both Bunnell and Poole note that many international school teachers equate their work with freedom and self-actualization rather than a loss of agency, just as Standing himself notes that labour market flexibility could be liberating. However, if the definition is essentially just about labour market legalities, then it is worth noting huge variability between international schools – because of their geographical situation and the legal frameworks that apply. After Brexit, international school teachers in Mainland Europe may be more highly protected than their colleagues back in the United States or the UK.

Therefore, although undoubtedly there may be countries or institutions in which this term is applicable, the blanket use of the term 'precariat' to describe international school teachers is highly problematic. Whilst international school teachers may not enjoy citizenship rights in the countries where they reside, as voluntary migrants their life situations cannot be compared to those of refugees and asylum seekers. Moreover, in many instances they enjoy an income and standard of living far in excess not only of the average citizen in their adopted country but also of those from their country of origin. Tarc et al.'s (2019) study of three families of Anglo-Western educators highlights the sense of agency that is clearly enjoyed by both the educators and their children, with, for example, the children able to access multiple systems of higher education and considerable travel opportunities afforded by their career. Similarly, the teachers in Poole's (2019b) study make it clear that they have economic privilege that they wouldn't enjoy as teachers working in their home countries.

The work of these theorists suggests that there are some teachers in some international schools who can be seen as part of the precariat, but this differs from country to country and school to school, and is subject to change. My own analysis of social media posts by international school educators demonstrates that a sense of precarity might have been heightened by the Covid-19 pandemic (Bailey, 2021). Poole (2019a) suggests it is teachers in Type C schools (Hayden & Thompson, 2013 – see above) who are most precarious; however, there are plenty of schools in this category who offer generous packages and security to their workers. It is true that international school teachers usually lack employment security, but so do expatriate CEOs and financial analysts. Indeed, the lives of teachers in many international schools are much closer to those of transnational business executives than of desperate economic migrants; in many locations, international school teachers will find their children hosting the birthday parties attended by the offspring of business executives, whilst economic migrants from developing countries are cleaning their kitchen – surely, it is the latter who are best termed 'the precariat'.

Indeed, there are other studies that suggest that international school educators may be part of the Global Middle Class, a far more elite group than the precariat, and which draw attention to the habitus of international school teachers to conceptualize their privilege. Teachers in international schools may enjoy more autonomy and status than they would receive in their home country (Bailey, 2015b), and as we saw in Chapter 2, there have been multiple attempts to theorize this advantage, using such terms as 'mobility capital', 'cosmopolitanism', 'resilience capital' and 'personal personhood'. It could be argued that international school teachers possess what Moret (2017) terms 'mobility capital' – a comfort with geographical movement and flexibility that is possessed only by a highly desirable elite (Kaufmann, Bergman & Joye, 2004). They are 'Anywheres'

(Goodhart, 2017), who are not bound by the geographically specific identities and allegiance to the familiar possessed by the 'Somewheres'. Poole (2019b) has also developed the concept of resilience capital. Based on a study of only three teachers working in China, he suggests that international teachers are often rich in this form of capital as a result of their experiences dealing with precarity. Poole and Bunnell (2020) posit that one instantiation of resilience capital is 'transition capital', an ability to deal with the constant job changes in international schools which have high teacher turnover and offer short-term contracts. Based on a study of teachers working at international schools in Melbourne (Australia), Blackmore (2014) argues that global educators have developed a professional habitus that enables them to be flexible and mobile – what she terms 'portable personhood'. Nevertheless, these teachers experienced a tension between their students' instrumental attitudes to education and their own educational ideals. In summary, many studies have suggested that international school teachers possess some form(s) of cultural capital that would lead to the conclusion that they are part of the Global Middle Class.

Tarc and Mishra Tarc (2015) are amongst those explaining how working in an international school can, in some contexts, draw teachers into a higher social class. They look at the position of Anglo-Western international school teachers working in the global south, arguing that these are 'middling' actors of mobility – neither the elite nor the impoverished, but working, colluding and colliding with those at the extremes of the class spectrum. Their experiences can be conflicted, Tarc and Mishra Tarc (2015) suggest, but equally their narratives can offer insights in the complex dynamics of group-making. They describe how their children and their social lives become entwined with those of the local elite:

> The social status of international school teachers may vary from country to country; in some societies they will be respected as 'intellectuals', whereas in others they will be treated as servants.
>
> (Tarc & Mishra Tarc, 2015: 206)

It would be disingenuous to pretend that there is not a racial dimension to this debate; the position of international school educators in part depends on their cultural and national origins. The Anglo-Western teachers in Tarc, Mishra Tarc and Wu's (2019) study belong to the Global Middle Class, which the authors define not as having a job outside of one's home country, but as developing the delocalized aspirations, the social belonging and the capital accumulation/transfer that characterizes this social group. These teachers develop cosmopolitan capital in their children just as they do in their students.

Tarc, Mishra Tarc and Wu (2019) chart how being an international school educator can give access to types of school choice as parents choose and change jobs in order to give their children entry into elite institutions they would be unable to afford in their country of origin. Their participants report having been able to accrue capital far beyond what would have been possible had they remained teaching in their country of origin. They also reported socializing with the elite of the country's where they lived; one participant recounted a tale involving multiple ambassadors, the governor and other local dignitaries. They reported encouraging their children to consider worldwide options for higher education. Whilst the participants differed in the extent to which they emphasized either networking possibilities or cross-cultural understanding as the main cultural benefits for their children, all stressed that they were accessing a superior education from their international schools.

Rey, Bolay and Gez (2020) suggest the term 'precarious privilege' to characterize the position of international school teachers, to encapsulate the idea that their jet-lagging travels are combined with economic insecurity. Based on a study of 'adventurer' teachers in international schools – those who are teaching overseas not because of a connection to the country or because they are trailing spouses of someone working in transnational corporations, but because they have actively chosen the international life – their study suggested that these are primarily Anglo-Saxon teachers who choose international school work to juggle a trade-off between lifestyle and finance. Although the image of international school teachers is that they are motivated primarily by a wish to travel, in fact most of their participants also had financial motivations for working in international schools. Many connected the wish to work overseas to payment of student debts. Others were seeking to save up for a house or retirement. Those early in their careers accepted employment flexibility in exchange for these benefits, and welcomed the chance to build up needed experience. For older/more senior teachers, economic precarity was more of an issue, as they became more expensive to employ and losing their job could often mean losing residency in a country they had lived for many years. Rey, Bolay and Gez's (2020) work, unlike that of previous authors, acknowledges the privilege that many international school teachers enjoy along with their financial insecurity.

Three examples of teachers I have met during different research studies provide insight into how teachers' identities and class positioning may be impacted by their work in international schools.

Example 1: Sheila

Sheila was a South African teacher at an international school in Malaysia, whom I met for my investigation into the experiences of host-country nationals in international schools (Bailey, 2015b). The majority of the students in her school were Malaysian.

She explained that she had chosen to work abroad to get herself out of her comfort zone working in a private school in South Africa.

She described how she had needed to change her teaching style since arriving at the school. First, she had discovered that her humour was not understood by her new students. Second, she no longer had to be as 'strict' as previously, as student behaviour was quite different. Third, she felt uncertain about what could and could not be said in the new environment:

> I'm definitely more aware of what I say here than I was in South Africa. Even though in South Africa, there could be a political history to it, in my class I wouldn't be worrying that I might say something that was insensitive. Whereas here, definitely.

In some ways, her account corresponds to theories of precarity, although she attributes this not to the risk of causing cultural offence rather than because her job is in general precarious:

> And also I think because it's a private school, and always at the back of your mind you're thinking, they could fire you, you know, you could lose your job if someone made that call. So I'm more cautious. But sometimes I wonder if cautious is the word or perhaps afraid. I do tend to play it much safer here than I would have.

Example 2: Sandra

Sandra was a teacher who participated in the same research study as Sheila. She was working at an international boarding school in Malaysia. As she couldn't drive, and the school was based in the countryside, she felt that she could never escape from work:

> Sometimes I feel like I don't rest because I go to work, I come home and my home is my work. So I've got all my laptop and everything on my dining-table. So during the week I don't really go out or getting away from it, so my productivity

is not as good as it could be, because I'm always doing bits. I'm always doing an email or a bit of marking. Because I never go away and come back fresh; it's always there. So I think if we were closer, or if we had opportunities to go out more, I'd take those breaks and come back a bit more productive. In the evenings and weekends.

Sandra's account of her work could be seen as supporting the notion that international school teachers are part of a global precariat; although she didn't feel that her work was insecure, she felt that she could not escape from it. However, that Sandra had previously left teaching in the UK because of stress, in order to work for a charity. It was the attraction of being able to travel with work and experience new places that had pulled her back into teaching. Her description of working life in international school suggested that she actually found it a less stressful environment than teaching in the UK:

> I really love [name of school]; I love the kids, the staff, I feel like I can relax here, I don't feel like it's a really pressurized environment, so I feel like I can do well in this kind of environment.

In other words, the difficulties associated with her work were due to the new cultural and social location, rather than the job itself. Sandra tried to capture the culture shock, explaining that she had 'gone to the middle of nowhere – from London to the middle of the jungle'.

Example 3: Greg

Greg was an American teacher working in China who participated in my research with Lucy Cooker into teaching identity in international schools (Bailey & Cooker, 2019). He is an example of the many teachers who have found work in international schools despite lacking teaching qualifications. However, his discussion does not resonate with theories of precarity, but rather suggests a sense of liberation. He had moved to China 'to change my life', without any background, interest or experience in education:

> I remember the first night when I was sitting in my bed and it was in this sort of cockroach invested little apartment. I looked up at the ceiling and there was a hole in the ceiling and I saw little tiny bugs crawling in and out of it. And I was lying there and thinking, I am 42 years old, I gave up a career to come to a country where I know no one, do not speak the language or read the language. Basically I am going to be a dish washer at some restaurant. At that moment I

thought that I had made a mistake, but it turns out that I didn't. I found a whole new career in mainstream education and I met a beautiful woman that became my wife.

He described feeling like a fake teacher at first, believing that he didn't really know anything apart from English. He described how that had slowly changed as he built up his experience, and that he was now pursuing a postgraduate qualification in education in order to get his experience and expertise validated.

Greg agreed that he was a Third Culture Teacher. Although he still felt American, and knew that others saw him as 'the big loud American', professionally he felt an affiliation to other international school teachers rather than to the teaching profession in the United States:

> These are people that have left their country and have basically branched out and gone to someplace new for them. They are accepting other cultures and they are living in it and they have accepted it. They are pliant and flexible people … and I admire them for the choices that they have made and those choices have brought them to the same place that I am today, and I see myself as very similar to those people. And it is funny because they are not Americans; they are Indians, they are Norwegians, they are Russians, and yet I feel so similar to them.

Conclusion

Globalization is making fundamental changes to the nature of work and professional identities. It is changing our affinities to place. Goodhart's (2017) work on the Anywheres and the Somewheres suggests that there is a schism in Western societies between the allegiances felt by elites and those felt by the excluded. Goodhart argues that this is causing fundamental political divisions that are reflected in recent elections and referenda in the UK, the United States and Western Europe. These schisms in how economies are developing are played out in international schools. International school teachers experience both a liberation and an anxiety as they see their scope of work being changed as a result of working in such institutions and their skills being both refined and redefined.

Globalization is not, however, a monolith. There are contradictory changes and competing tensions in the changes that are taking place. Not all international school educators are being affected in the same way or at the same pace. Our discussion has suggested that Anglophone educators, qualified or not, may not have the same vulnerability to increased workload and erosion of professional status as some of their colleagues. I return to discussion of inequalities within international schools in Chapter 7.

What we have seen in this chapter are possibilities for seismic change in the work and the social status of teachers – for both the better and the worse. Those working in international education are on the cusp of fundamental shifts in the nature and value of teaching. This is a particularly fertile ground for understanding the impact of globalization on a range of workers, but particularly on those who are given responsibility for the education of students worldwide.

5

Internationalism or Westernization?

Introduction

International schooling originated in the needs of predominantly Western parents seeking academic opportunities for their children without the need to send them back to their passport country for schooling. The extent to which those Western origins continue to flavour contemporary international schools has been an increasing concern of researchers over the past twenty years. Commentators have sought to evaluate the extent to which international schools offer a form of neocolonialist education. They have theorized how and why, when most international educators aver a commitment to cultural diversity and equality, Western approaches have continued to dominate at least some international schools. The preceding chapter considered the teachers in international schools; in this chapter we turn to looking at learners and learning in international schools. Specifically, I consider the extent to which the internationalization of schooling constitutes a form of covert Westernization.

In the discussion below, I examine the relationship between the local and the Western in international schools, acknowledging that different types of schools have merged these in different ways. Three aspects of the local context are identified – social values and behaviours; local cultures of teaching and learning; and local language(s). I use the term 'local' rather than 'national' to acknowledge that the school's community may not be representative of the nation more generally. For example, the 'local' for an international school in Malaysia may be the Chinese Malaysians who dominate the school, rather than the Malay ethnicity that is the majority nationally. The 'local' for an international school in Bahrain may be the Sunni Muslims who attend the school (and constitute the more affluent sector of society), rather than the Shia Muslims who constitute the majority nationally. It is important in discussing the 'local' to avoid implicitly homogenizing the nation in which a school is situated.

I consider whether Westernization has been resisted/rejected by schools, teachers and students in international schools. Thereafter, I look at the burgeoning literature drawing stakeholders' attention to the importance of examining their own preconceptions. In other words, there is emerging evidence of growing self-critique in international school circles over such forms of Westernization, especially in schools where the majority of students are from non-Western backgrounds. This critique has been a consequence of the increasing number of host-country nationals in international schools.

In my previous writings on this subject, I identified three tensions concerning the nature and purpose of international schools resulting from the increasing numbers of host country nationals in Asia attending these schools (Bailey, 2018). I suggested that schools with large number of host country nationals encountered: conflicting regulatory frameworks (national authorities versus international assessment organizations); conflicting educational values; and conflicting social values. Here, I will consider the cultural complexities of international schooling both for schools dominated by host country nationals and for schools in which there is more student cultural diversity.

The concepts of the Third Culture Kid (TCK) and the Global Nomad have been developed to capture the lack of belonging and sense of alienation from their own culture that some students feel as a result of their international schooling (Useem & Downie, 1976; Fail, Thompson & Walker, 2004; Langford, 2012; Tanu, 2017). The Third Culture Kid inhabits neither their home culture nor the culture where they reside, but a third space, shared with other TCKs. 'TCK' is a broad term that could apply to children whose parents migrated to a country where they are now permanently settled. By contrast, the Global Nomad is a child whose parents have relocated overseas for employment for a significant part of their childhood, and therefore refers more specifically to non-host-country nationals in international schools.

There is an extensive literature exploring the cultural challenges that students may face in international schools (Grimshaw & Sears, 2008; Tanu, 2017) which focuses on issues around identity, belonging and the role of language. This makes an important contribution to understanding how individuals negotiate the world of international schooling, but the focus in this book is to employ critical theory to understand the structural effects in terms of social inequalities. In this respect, these terms silence as much as they empower; both terms imply there is a kind of equality in this mobility, that all children whose parents work abroad will experience similar levels of dislocation. By contrast, the empirical evidence suggests that in traditional international schools serving expatriate communities the cultural dissonance is greater for students who do not come from Anglo-American backgrounds (Allan, 2002, 2003; Fitzsimons, 2019). In addition, the students in schools predominantly serving host-country nationals may still reside in their home culture, but experience cultural dissonance as they move between the cultures of home and school (Bailey, 2015a; Frangie, 2017). In other words, systematic inequalities are ignored by the implied migratory democracy of this terminology. The focus on this chapter is to highlight these systematic inequalities.

I begin by exploring the relationship between the global/international and the Western in the world of the international school.

Global or Western?

Hughes (2020a) points to the two very different ways of understanding the mission of being international. First, there is the international school with a curriculum focused on development of international values, community service and respect for diversity in order to make the world a better place. Second, there is the international school with a curriculum focused on taking diverse student populations, offering them a Western curriculum, and ensuring that they have the language (usually English) and skills to enter a US or UK university. Hughes examines some mission statements from international schools about their connections with local communities, concluding that terms 'international community' and 'local community' are devoid of real meaning, and concluding that

> the feeling that emanates from these statements, not intended but somehow palpable, is that the local community is the recipient of acts of charity, a backwater community still wallowing in the twentieth century who, if they are lucky, might expect a visit from the star-studded international jet set.
>
> (Hughes, 2020a: 182)

The methodology used to select these mission statements and to analyse them is unclear; Hughes's account is a piece of rhetoric written by an international school insider rather than a systematic piece of research. However, his account offers some insights into competing relationships between the local and the international, and provides a good summary of the Westernization thesis of international schooling.

The progressive approach and the neoliberal approach are two very different ways of conceptualizing the international school curriculum. The former takes international schools at face value, as offering a curriculum focused on ensuring that students can strive for a better world. The latter suggests that the international school curriculum responds to the market and that the market at the moment wants an elite, Western education. There is some empirical evidence to support the latter view. Although the international school typically affirms its commitment to cultural equality and is committed to affirming the identities and cultures of its students, several ethnographic studies have suggested there are multiple ways in which appeals to the 'global' can serve as a covert form of Westernization.

For example, in the two international schools in Belgium and Serbia studied by Fitzsimons (2019), the school curriculum and culture inadvertently created a hierarchy of identities, with Anglo-Western identities at the top. Although the students identified parts of the curriculum in which they could explore their national and international identities (primarily, language learning, history and enquiry-based learning), students from non-Anglophone communities were sometimes marginalized socially. Moreover, although the students discussed the importance of multilingualism to being international, some found themselves losing their first language as they acquired English fluency. The students welcomed learning about different histories, and appreciating other perspectives on history, but some were concerned that they were not learning their own national history. Fitzsimons concludes that Western identities dominated the schools. English was the language that received most emphasis, Western historical narratives received the most attention and Western values permeated classrooms. In fact, one participant went so far as to claim that 'international' had become synonymous with 'American'. Fitzsimons emphasizes that this definition of 'international' was not created by international schools but reflects Western dominance of society. However, the schools failed to critique this account (Fitzsimons, 2019).

Similarly, Allan (2002, 2003) employed a case study of an international school in the Netherlands to show how even in international education a single culture can predominate, to the detriment of minority and majority students alike. Allan's ethnography explores how the students responded to the loss of face some experienced in encounters at the school. Students coming from Anglo-American backgrounds experienced little or no cultural dissonance when entering the school, but students from other cultural backgrounds experienced considerable cultural dissonance. For the former, little intercultural learning took place; for the latter, the shock could be severe, and students varied in their response, with some becoming ethnocentric, whilst others sought to assimilate. He argues that intercultural learning is often left to luck rather than systematically planned.

Other researchers have drawn attention to how Western identities are constructed as for sale in particular international schools. Bunnell (2008b) examines the prestigious English public schools who are opening overseas campuses or franchised campuses across Asia. He argues that these schools are 'glocalized' – in other words, the international brand name of the well-known English school is given a local flavour, and their schooling is sold to the local elite. Ironically, Bunnell suggests that the schools were originally motivated to establish these campuses by a need to convince the UK Charity Commission of their philanthropic nature for tax exemption purposes. The profit gained from Asian elites is used to fund scholarships in the UK.

Drawing on his experience as an international school leader in Dubai, Al Farra (2012) argues that there is no intrinsic conflict between the IB's conception of internationalism and Arabic culture, but that in practice international schools sometimes present a Westernized schooling to their students. For instance Western role models are used extensively, and little attention is given to Islamic Studies and the Arabic language, which results in Arabic culture being devalued.

In the following section, I unravel the ways in which Westernization can inadvertently occur by identifying three aspects of 'local' culture that researchers have shown may be in conflict with the culture of an international school.

Local and 'Global' Cultures of International Schooling

In this section, I discuss three dimensions of local culture that may be in tension with the implicitly Western assumptions and assumptions of an international school: cultural values and assumptions; cultures of teaching and learning; and linguistic dimensions of culture.

Cultural values and assumptions

Cultural values and assumptions permeate any institution; in an international school which may be largely staffed and led by Western teachers, yet attended by non-Western or diverse students, this can result in a dissonance between the 'international' and the local. Some of the examples highlighted by researchers include attitudes to religious and other forms of knowledge (Burke, 2015; Cooker et al., 2015), beliefs about gender difference (Frangie, 2017), assumptions about roles and responsibilities within the family (Frangie, 2017) and attitudes to different members of a community (Stevenson et al., 2017).

Knowledge is socially constructed and what is deemed legitimate knowledge by Western teachers may differ from the knowledge and ways of knowing that are valorized by other cultures. For instance, Burke (2015) describes the cultural emphasis on religion and importance given to bush medicine that impacts on science teaching in The Bahamas.

Frangie (2017) details some of the cultural differences between Qatari culture and the culture of a case study international school in Qatar from the perspective of Grade 6 students. The students felt uncomfortable with the emphasis on co-education of their Western teachers, which conflicted with the gender segregation from puberty onwards that is normal in Qatar. Furthermore, they did not feel that their teachers understood that they must respect parental authority within their culture. Moreover, some students noted that they had responsibilities at school whereas at home they had nannies and a driver to organize them.

Our study of prosocial education commissioned by the IB focused on what the IB calls 'Caring' – the consideration and action taken towards other people, including those less fortunate than yourself. However, at the case study schools my colleagues and I visited in Indonesia and Singapore, this terminology was rejected and teachers and leaders argued that 'Respect' would be a term that resonated better with local cultures (Stevenson et al., 2015). In other words, Confucian Heritage and Western cultures seemed to conceptualize prosocial behaviour differently.

These cultural conflicts are not just a question of difference, but take place in a context of power imbalances in wider society. As a consequence, the Western can be constructed in the school community as the universal, and the non-Western as the provisional or problematic. This is illustrated by Emenike and Plowright's (2017) study of Nigerian students at two Nigerian international schools negotiating the contrasting cultural settings of international school and home. The students encountered a range of cultural differences, for example, over the way that children are expected to behave in the presence of adults. However, Emenike and Plowright (2012) found that whilst the students used their critical thinking skills to challenge their home environments they were more reluctant to use them to challenge the Western culture of the school. The researchers employ the term 'Third Culture Indigenous Kids' to capture the relationship between these host-country students and their neocolonial educational environments.

Cultures of teaching and learning

In addition to general differences in culture, the expectations of teaching and learning that teachers, students and parents bring to international schools are socially constructed and hence vary by culture. The increase in host-country nationals attending international schools in Asia makes it particularly important to note the well-documented differences between Asian and Western cultures in their approaches to learning (Li, 2005). Jin and Cortazzi (2006) suggest the term 'cultures of learning' to capture the unspoken assumptions about learning – about how effective learning takes place and what constitutes evidence that learning that has occurred – that may vary between cultures. One example of how Western and Confucian Heritage cultures see learning in different ways are the contrasting role given to talk in the classroom (Jin & Cortazzi, 2006). In Western classrooms, teachers encourage students to articulate their point of view and discuss the teacher's assertions in a critical manner; in Confucian Heritage cultures, it is believed that learning happens best when the students listen carefully and respect the teacher's authority. An absence of student talk may be taken as a lack of student engagement by a Western teacher, but intended as evidence of engagement by Asian students.

Research suggests that Western approaches to teaching and learning have become valorized in some international schools as somehow representing best educational practice. Burke's (2015) work, although not specific to international schooling, illustrates this. During her fieldwork on science teaching in the Caribbean, she noted that whilst the Caribbean teachers expressed respect for British teachers' knowledge and skills, this was not reciprocated. The British teachers averred that they were so esteemed that they could talk nonsense and still be believed. Interestingly, the students did not concur with this assumption; they saw their British teachers as no-nonsense and cold, and also as lacking the religious framework that local teachers possessed.

A Western conception of what it means to be learner-centred cannot be easily transferred to a non-Western context, where student may not expect, or be accustomed to, learner autonomy. Although Awang, Cheah and Chua's (2020) study of a government school in Malaysia using the IB Diploma Programme was not conducted in a school that describes itself as 'international', it provides ample evidence of how tensions between international and local ways of teaching and learning are experienced by teachers and students. The teachers in the study explain the challenges they face in using the DP; they describe the language struggles of students as well as the need for teachers to familiarize themselves with a teaching approach that encourages more learner independence and the learner-centred activities in the classroom. Similarly, Deveney (2005) explores how the expatriate teachers at her case study international school in Thailand believed that Thai culture influenced their Thai pupils. She finds that the teachers reported needing to adjust their teaching methods to accommodate the different behaviours and expectations of the predominantly Thai students at the school. Parental expectations of education also vary by culture. The school leaders interviewed in Lee, Hallinger and Walker's (2012) study of IB schools in Asia reported a tension between parental academic expectations and the IB's educational philosophy. For example, the Asian parents placed a high value on the study of maths and science, whereas the educators placed more emphasis on student interest and motivation. The Western leaders in Lee, Hallinger and Walker's (2012) study considered their approach to facilitate 'deep learning', implying that they thought Asian approaches to teaching and learning to be inferior.

A further example of these conflicting educational values concerns the role of memorization in Islamic contexts. In our study of the IB's Middle Years Programme in the UAE, my colleagues and I found that some teachers of Arabic origins argued that there was a conflict between the expectations of the IB and the importance their culture placed on memorization of the Quran. One participant said that memorization was 'forbidden' by the IB, which mandated that inquiry-led approaches should be used instead, whereas recitation of the Quran is an essential part of Islamic studies. In some of the schools we visited, especially those which served the Emirati community, this was explicitly seen as a tension between East and West (Stevenson et al., 2017).

Memorization of the Quran also features as an issue in Adly Gamal's (2020) study of teachers of Islamic studies in a case study international school in Qatar. Adly Gamal suggests that when Islamic Studies teachers work in a Western milieu international school that devalues memorization, they may not be seen as competent teachers. In addition, the international school environment seemed to place little value on their role in transmission of Islamic knowledge. The participants in the study felt that their subject was undervalued by many parents, who rarely inquired into children's achievement in Islamic Studies and placed more value on children acquiring English and the other skills needed for entrance to Western universities. Adly Gamal suggests that as a result of these cultural differences and the devaluing of the knowledge they communicated, the teachers came to see their role primarily as spiritual advisors and confidants, rather than simply as subject experts.

In addition to these cultural differences in academic learning, holistic aspects of education are often contested in international schools. This is unsurprising since holistic education pays attention to the development of character and interpersonal skills, both of which are inherently related to cultural norms about social relationships. For example, when I was part of a research team studying wellbeing at international schools in Asia, Europe and the Americas for the IB, my colleagues and I found that schools experienced competing ideas of well-being and of how student behaviour should be viewed amongst their stakeholders. In Thailand, one senior leader explained that Thai parents believed that spiritual well-being was paramount, whereas spirituality was not necessarily a focus of Western educators. In China, Asian parents and Western educators sometimes had conflicting beliefs about the role of corporal punishment in supporting effective learning (Cooker et al., 2015).

There are, then, a number of ways in which both the academic and non-academic expectations of teaching and learning may differ between cultures, and there is substantial evidence that Western educators may exclude or denigrate non-Western approaches as an inadvertent consequence of establishing what they believe to be best practice. Conversely, in my research studies I have encountered misconceptions about conflicting educational values based on Western stereotypes of 'the Other'. For example, in our study of the MYP in the UAE, Western teachers told us that the IB's emphasis on the importance of being open-minded was in conflict with local values. By contrast, teachers from the Arab Region informed us that being open-minded was emphasized in the Quran (Stevenson et al., 2017).

1. Linguistic dimensions of culture

Although international schools usually have multilingual communities, in practice they often function as a monolingual habitus (Burr, 2018). The emphasis on many institutions is on fluency in English, with little attention to maintaining other languages, and there can be an inadvertent devaluing of home language and, by implication, culture. Englishness – both linguistic and cultural – is sold as a means of ensuring distinction in university applications (Gardner-McTaggart, 2018a). As a result, other languages – and the cultural norms that are embedded in language – are silenced.

In the world of the international school, all languages are equal but some are more equal than others. In addition, not all variants of English are accorded equal status. Gardner-McTaggart's (2018a) research on the leaders of IB schools demonstrates that they draw on high-status variants of English, from the Anglophone countries. The rationale for this dominance is that it enables access to elite universities in the UK and the United States. English is thereby asserted as a form of symbolic power, and a number of researchers have discussed how other languages and non-dominant variants of English are excluded or marginalized in international schools (Allan, 2002; Al Farra, 2012; Fitzsimons, 2019; Gardner-McTaggart, 2018a).

Example: Bahraini Parents in Bahrain

In my study of Bahraini parents using international schools in Bahrain, a recurrent theme of the interviews, focus groups and open survey responses was concern about their child's loss of the Arabic language and Arabic culture. In addition, many parents were worried about they saw specifically as Westernization; elements of Westernization included styles of clothing and exposure to members of the opposite sex. Some of the concerns raised were about children being exposed to material that was considered immoral in Bahraini culture, that their behaviour could be misjudged by others and about the difficulties they would face in integrating into Bahraini workplaces in the future. For example, Bahraini culture largely segregates men and women, and parents were concerned that international schools introduced children to non-Bahraini values concerning adolescent relationships and homosexuality. Another worry was that in the future their child might be friendly to a colleague of the opposite sex, which could be open to misinterpretation. However, whilst they raised these concerns in discussion, these were not complaints directed against the school; the parents felt that responsibility for addressing these cultural differences did not lie with the school. Rather, it was their own responsibility to instil Islamic values and to maintain their first language.

The parents made it clear that they had cosmopolitan aspirations for their children, wishing them to be comfortable with moving in diverse cultural settings and dealing with people from all over the world, whilst at the same time retaining their Arab identity. As a result, they were pleased that their children were learning to function in a different cultural milieu. Although they did not want their children to be Westernized, an ability to manage Western settings was in fact the point of sending them to international schools. One focus group regretted their school's decision not to celebrate Christmas out of cultural sensitivity, scoffing the idea that it would impact on their Islamic identity. One parent explained:

> I wanted my children to start with an international school to get exposed to international cultures. The teachers – I wanted them to be from different countries, different cultures. And the children next to them in the classroom, I didn't want it to be only Bahrainis or only Arabs or only British. I wanted them to be exposed to all of them. And to be part of a bigger world, at the end.

Resisting Westernization?

The literature studied above points to a growing awareness of the dangers of covert Westernization in international schools. Indeed, studies of the impact of IB programmes on teaching and learning – frequently commissioned by the IB themselves – recurrently point to two challenges for schools in reconciling the national and the international: first, the need to adhere to national regulations (for example, relating to curriculum or assessment) and second, varying cultural expectations about teaching and learning (Dickson, Perry & Ledger, 2018).

As a result of this growing sensitivity, several researchers have discussed the ways in which educators can resist or reject the inadvertent Westernization of international schooling. Fitzsimons (2019) asserts that enquiry-based learning 'has the ability to serve as a culturally responsive practice within a culturally relevant pedagogy' (Fitzsimons, 2019: 285). Wickins and Edwards (2018) use the metaphor of a Green Tea Frappuccino at a Starbucks to describe the contemporary international school in Malaysia – in other words, a local twist on a global brand. Drawing on the idea of 'glocalization' – how a global brand is given a twist to appeal to a local market – they try to make sense of how international schools fit within their local contexts. Wickins and Edwards propose a self-evaluation exercise that international schools can undertake to judge the extent to which the education they provide includes a local as well as an international dimension. They call for schools to consider whether they show their commitment to the local through their school values and mission; their recruitment policies; their curriculum, including attitudes to language; and their local community engagement.

Burke (2017) powerfully recounts her own attempt as an expatriate teacher to deliver a lesson with locally relevant content, and the students' rejection of local knowledge in favour of what they needed to know for a test that would give them access to university overseas. Through analysis of this critical incident, she argues that both the material taught and the pedagogies employed by expatriate teachers are culturally situated and suggests:

> Teachers need to understand the complexities of being invited into a given context as a representative of a globalised knowledge network, and make efforts to understand how to enact equitable practices and behaviours without marginalising, subjugating or belittling the learner's culturally-situated beliefs and ways of knowing.
>
> (Burke, 2017: 217)

For Burke, postcolonial theory can be used to critically examine the position of the Western expatriate teacher in countries that were formally colonies. She suggests that expatriate teachers need to consciously deconstruct how their own background has impacted on their relationship towards the knowledge they teach, and to explore their relationship to local forms of knowing.

These well-intentioned accounts are united in their assumption that the responsibility lies with expatriate teachers and leaders to avoid their inadvertent Westernization of their international school students, in other words, they come perilously close to a rewriting of the time-honoured white saviour narrative. By contrast, other studies have focused on a more agentic interpretation of why students and parents from diverse cultures may choose an apparently Westernized education. These studies recognize that many of the individuals making those choices are not oppressed and marginalized, but in fact occupy positions of privilege and power within their own cultures, and attempt to conceptualize their choices in this light.

For example, Waters (2007) argues that some parents may be self-consciously fusing contrasting cultural traditions as part of their attempts to gain educational advantage for their children. The parents Waters studies in Hong Kong seek to nurture a mixture of Western and Chinese traits in their children, in order for them to acquire the specific identity and habitus of 'overseas-educated local'.

The conscious deployment of Western narratives to resist restricted versions of national identity is also seen in De Silva, Woods and Kong's (2020) study of a Christian international school in China which operates underground and illegally owing to the proscription on providing religious-focused schooling. They explain how the school integrates Christianity and Confucianism and draws on Western culture to construct an alternative version of school to the Communist, secular context. De Silva, Woods and Kong (2020) explain that some of the cultural choices made by the school are forced – for example, because it operates illegally, the school is unable to offer the kind of patriotic field trips that are usual in Chinese government schools. Yet, an alternative version of national identity also features within this school community; whilst the school focuses on transmitting international (largely, American) culture to students to prepare them for non-Chinese universities (either overseas or in China), it also teaches Chinese language, history and geography. It seems, then, that there are contexts in which the marginalization of national narratives by a Western version of being international may affirm certain cultural identities and not always serve to exclude.

Teachers, too, may feel empowered by reconceptualizing their role in an international context. In Adly Gamal's (2020) study from Qatar, although we have seen that the teachers of Islamic Studies felt their subject expertise was devalued by the international school, there were other ways in which they compared their current positioning favourably to their previous roles in national (government) schools. Specifically, they reported that teacher autonomy to make pedagogical decisions was respected in the less authoritarian international school environment.

In summary, Western norms and local cultures do not always conflict, and a more nuanced interpretation of the relationship that stakeholders coming from non-Western backgrounds may have with Western narratives of nationalism is needed.

Example: Host-Country Nationals in an International School in Malaysia

In my case study of a school serving predominantly host-country nationals in Malaysia (Bailey, 2015a), I contrasted Malaysina student and expatriate teacher perceptions of the school. The three tensions identified above between Malaysian culture and Western norms featured in their contrasting accounts.

Both staff and students questioned whether the school was 'really' international because of its strong Malaysian flavour, but for the teachers the question was whether the school lived up to their high ideals of internationalism, whereas the students sought to distance the school from the elitism they associated with international schools. The teachers agonized about the impact of English medium on the students' cultural identities whereas the students viewed the language instrumentally as enabling them to access university education overseas.

Staff and students both reported differences between Western and Malaysian approaches to teaching and learning. The students cited differences in teaching such as the skills focused upon in the classroom and the forms of discipline employed. The expatriate teachers assumed that their approaches to teaching were superior to those of local teachers, whereas the students reported valuing both approaches. The Malaysian students felt that both groups of teachers could learn from one another, whereas the expatriate teachers suggested simply that the Malaysian teachers needed further training. Although the expatriate teachers spoke about adapting their teaching style since arriving at the school, they had learnt from experience rather than their Malaysian colleagues. Although some teachers were aware that students valued their Malaysian colleagues, they assumed this was because students found it easier to be 'spoon-fed' (Bailey, 2015a).

The expatriate teachers also discussed some of the approaches to learning that they found unusual in Malaysian students. They mentioned their high levels of self-motivation in the classroom, their focus on academic attainment, their reluctance to challenge the teacher with their own opinions and their discomfort with making mistakes. The students were aware that the school was changing them as learners, feeling that they had become more open-minded, more willing to debate issues and less focused on their grades.

Three aspects of culture that emerged from the data analysis were cultural uncertainty, culture shock and Malaysian cultural identity. Both staff and students reported initial uncertainty when first arriving at the school; neither group knew what was permissible in this new environment. Both groups reported having experienced culture shock when first arriving at the school. There were differences between individuals in how they conceptualized Malaysian cultural identity, however. For the teachers, this was threatened by the school. By contrast, the students were divided. One student cautioned against an outdated view of Malaysian culture rooted in the rural past, whereas another felt that she had been Westernized.

Conclusion

This chapter has critically analysed the thesis that international schools proffer a form of Westernization and that the avowed internationalism of their curriculum and institutional norms is in fact embedded in Western norms. I have explored the complex relationship between international schools and the local cultures in which they are embedded, identifying three areas of potential conflict: the general cultural values and norms that infuse the school organization, culturally different approaches to teaching in learning and linguistic dimensions of culture that may be overlooked in the English-medium environment of an international school.

I have cautioned against an approach that suggests that non-Western students (or their parents) need Western help in resisting such narratives of internationalism. Complexity and ambivalence characterize the critical studies that have examined these tensions. We have seen that cosmopolitan aspirations may lead some parents and students to engage with Western institutions whilst remaining uncomfortable with the consequences of this choice, whilst other parents and students exercise agency through the fusion of cultures, constructing an elite identity that distinguishes them both from others in their locality and from Western identities. International schooling thereby provides a site in which the relationship between elements of the national and the Western in the process of globalization is contested.

A more detailed analysis of the curricula used in international schools and their contribution to the reproduction of such inequalities constitutes the focus of the next chapter.

6

Educating for Global Citizenship

Introduction

Over the preceding chapters, I have explored in detail particular aspects of what is occurring inside international schools. In so doing, I have conceptualized international schools not just as a system of macro-inequalities, but as microsites in which power and privilege are enacted (Ball, 1987). In this chapter, I continue this approach as the curriculum is examined as a site of cultural and social reproduction.

There is no homogeneous international school curriculum, although there are commonalities between the various curricula choices such schools make. The chapter begins by considering the range of curricula available for use in international schools and provides an overview of the use of these curricula – and their attendant forms of assessment – in different cultural settings. The appeal of 'British' [sic] forms of assessment (iGCSEs and A levels), American high school diplomas and international curricula (the programmes of the IBO or the IPC, for instance) is examined as reflecting different philosophies of what it means to be educated, and of who is to judge education. These in turn are seen as both creating and reproducing inequalities within national contexts, for example, by reinforcing Western ways of seeing the world or by legitimating other existing social inequalities. We look specifically at the concept of international-mindedness that is purported to be central to international schooling in order to understand this.

It is suggested that these curricula can either reinforce or undermine national values, national priorities and the existing social order within a particular nation. The curriculum can therefore be a contested site in which tensions between the 'international' and the national are played out. The chapter draws extensively on our research in the UAE, and elsewhere, in order to illustrate these points, during which we have seen 'two masters' (the IBO and the local authorities) creating tensions for schools endeavouring to meet the demands of both international values and national systems of governance. The introduction by PISA of an additional measure to its suite of assessments, 'Global Competence' demonstrates that these tensions are equally applicable to national systems of schooling. It is argued that examination of international schooling provides a useful site for exploring explicitly these tensions that remain latent in government schools.

Finally, we examine assessment in international contexts, looking at how international qualifications have legitimated social inequalities, but conversely how the Covid-19 pandemic left international qualifications uncertain and may lead to a reassertion of the national in the assessment of education.

The Curriculum in International Schools

The International Baccalaureate (IB) was founded in 1968 in order to offer programmes and assessment for international schools. The IB differs from many national systems of education because of its explicit commitment to character education throughout the 3–19 age range, through its Learner Profile, a series of ten character traits that the IB programmes seek to develop. Together, these ten traits are claimed to epitomize 'international-mindedness', one of the distinctive foci of the programmes. For younger learners, the IB takes an inquiry, cross-curricular approach to concept-based learning, and these elements remain key, though changing in manifestation, as a child progresses through its programmes. By the time the student reaches the DP, the programme is disciplinary-focused, but interdisciplinary elements, such as the study of Theory of Knowledge, remain. Although the programmes of the International Baccalaureate (IB) have framed much of what is written about the curriculum in relation to international schooling, in fact many schools that denote themselves as 'international' follow other programmes. In addition, the IB is now followed in large numbers of national schools worldwide.

There are other programmes, for example, that have been designed specifically for international education. Walker (2016) discusses three international curricula that predated the IB, specifically those developed at the International School of Geneva, the United Nations International School in New York and Atlantic College in Wales. He identifies common elements that he suggests constitute aspects of a 'truly' international curriculum – an ethos that values international understanding, attention to language development, a willingness to engage with contentious issues and a commitment to making the world a better place. He suggests that the International Baccalaureate programmes similarly adhere to these elements.

More recently, Fieldwork Education launched the International Primary Curriculum (IPC) in 2000, which is now used in over 1000 schools in more than ninety countries (Fieldwork Education, 2020). The same organization has subsequently developed international curriculum programmes for early years and middle years as well. This curriculum also aspires to develop 'international-mindedness' in young people. Fieldwork Education is now part of Nord Anglia, an international corporation that owns sixty-six international schools across the world at the time of writing, and which targets the 'premium' segment of the international schools market.

Some researchers, such as Bunnell, Fertig and James (2016), see following an international curriculum as the defining feature of a true international school; others have taken a more critical approach to this construction of being international (Bolay & Rey, 2020), which we discuss further below. Certainly, many schools which are avowedly international follow a national curriculum, usually one from a country other than the one where they are located. For example, an international school in Malaysia may follow the Australian curriculum, the French curriculum or award an American high school Diploma.

Sometimes, such international schools have a clear national allegiance and adhere to the curriculum requirements they would have to adhere to in that other nation (rather than the country in which they are situated). For example, many schools around the world declare themselves to be British schools and follow the English National Curriculum throughout all years. In practice, however, this does not mean that the students are receiving the same curricular experience as students based in the UK. The iGCSEs and international A levels offered by Cambridge International and Pearson Edexcel, for example, are loosely modelled on the English qualifications of the same name, but there are salient differences. Whilst the qualifications have been benchmarked against English national qualifications, and are generally recognized as equivalent by international universities, they are not subject to the same regulations. Cambridge International avers that it needs to differ, in response to the needs of the multicultural and multilingual institutions that are taking its qualifications. Coursework requirements, texts studied, grading and the use of modular assessment are all ways in which the international curriculum and assessment differ from the national equivalents.

Moreover, at other times, the national connection is more tenuous. Many international schools opt to take iGCSEs and international A levels as culminating assessments, but this does not mean that they are following the English National Curriculum with younger age groups. Conversely, in some 'British' schools, students may be able to opt for the IB Diploma Programme instead of A levels for their last two years of 'British' education.

In addition, in many contexts, international schools may face national curriculum requirements that they need to reconcile with whatever international curriculum they follow. So, for example, there may be religious education, national language or other regulations. Schools may need to work towards national and international assessments concurrently. For example, for our research study on the IB Primary Years Programme Exhibition (the culminating study and assessment of the primary school years), we visited schools in Russia which were simultaneously following the inquiry-based cross-curricular PYP as they prepared students for knowledge-focused, subject-specific national exams (Medwell et al., 2017).

There are a variety of curricula that are used by international schools, and we are wary of generalizing across different schools and contrasting national contexts. However, one key point that is typically true is that international schools have far more latitude in their choice of curriculum and forms of assessment than their national counterparts. At the same time, they may face competing pressures – for example, from government regulations, parental expectations – that mean they are essentially juggling contradictory curricular demands. An exploration of the contradictions schools face and how they see to balance them is the focus of most of this chapter.

Another commonality across many schools is the use of curriculum and assessment from Western, Anglophone contexts in international schools in diverse cultural contexts. In other words, the judgement of who is educated is being displaced from non-Western nations to Western centres of assessment, in what can be seen as assessment imperialism. We begin by analysing the concept of the curriculum, identifying the many roles that have been claimed for a curriculum, and critically appraising what it means to be an international curriculum.

Conceptualizing the International School Curriculum

In his seminal work on the curriculum, Wiliam (2013) identifies four major aims for the curriculum: personal empowerment, cultural transmission, preparation for citizenship and preparation for work. However, aside from personal empowerment, all of these aims are problematized by an international context: transmission of whose culture? Preparation for global or national citizenships? Preparation to work where?

The curriculum is contested even in government schools worldwide. However, this is exacerbated in international schools – for what society are students being prepared? In national schools, the employment market, the culture context and the national identity for which the child is being prepared may be contested but have at least some demarcation; in international schools, the purpose of the curriculum is far less clear. For what society are students being prepared, for what job market, to function in what cultural setting? In addition, there may be tensions between different aspects of the curriculum, with the taught curriculum differing from the assessed curriculum, and the hidden curriculum (what is implicitly taught by schools) perhaps being of greater importance than either of these.

A superficial response would be to suggest that international curricula follow international best practice, that they somehow distil the best of what we have learnt about how children learn and what they should know. Critical theorists have, however, critiqued this narrative. For example, Stobie (2016) questions whether there is such a thing as 'international best practice' that can be used to develop the curriculum for such schools, suggesting instead that curriculum must be constructed locally to meet the needs of a specific institution in a particular context. In other words, Stobie's approach problematizes the importation of Western-developed programmes into very different contexts.

Stobie (2016) asks what the rising number of host-country nationals attending international schools in many parts of the Asia means for the curriculum, and highlights some of the challenges of introducing an international (or non-national) curriculum. Stobie contrasts Western and Confucian approaches to teaching to learning, arguing that the former adheres to the Socratic tradition of inquiry with the teacher as facilitator whereas the latter places more emphasis on the transmission of knowledge with the teacher as a source of wisdom. Stobie also draws attention to the importance of assessment practices to curriculum practices, noting that in Confucian cultures the focus is on preparing students for an examination. The teacher's role in such contexts is to prepare students for the examination rather than to summatively assess them, and therefore giving teachers responsibility for assessment of coursework sits uneasily in this tradition. Although Stobie attempts to establish principles to guide the implementation of an international curriculum in such schools, this is the least convincing part of his work. For example, he suggests that an emphasis on global-mindedness is essential, but doesn't define or exemplify this beyond saying that first languages other than English must be maintained. We return to the concept of 'international-mindedness' in the following section.

Discussion of such issues has dominated discussion of the curriculum in international schools, and underpins our critical analysis below. We shall see that several commentators have, like Gardner-McTaggart (2016), drawn on the writings of Pierre Bourdieu to suggest that the IB programmes offer symbolic capital and distinction to their graduates. For Bourdieu (1998), a person's position and status in society are not simply determined by their economic capital (or wealth), but by their social and cultural capital – the many elements that give them advantage and route to a higher social status, such as knowledge, ways of thinking and manner of presenting oneself to the world, and which are developed by elite forms of education. Symbolic capital refers to resources that are conferred on an individual on the basis of their prestige – Gardner-McTaggart (2016) applies this approach to the case of international education, suggesting that possession of the IB Diploma may be recognized as particularly high status for a range of reasons.

In order to understand how a curriculum may achieve this, Bourdieu's work can be complemented by that of Bernstein (1975). According to Bernstein, a curriculum establishes a relationship between different forms of knowledge. In some curricula, there is a strict separation between subjects, which Bernstein terms 'strong classification'. Similarly, within a subject knowledge may be hierarchically ordered (what Bernstein calls strong framing). In other curricula, connections may be drawn between subjects or cross-curricular approaches may dominate (weak classification), and student-led study may mean that students encounter areas of knowledge in an unpredictable order (weak framing). Bernstein (1975) explores how curricula may differ according to whether they have strong framing and strong classification between different areas of knowledge (the collection code) or have weak classification and weak framing (the integrated code). Bernstein notes that the new middle class in the UK had a preference for weaker framing. Integrating this work with that of Bourdieu, we can understand the integrated code as being a form of intellectual inquiry that has status in globalized knowledge societies. Similarly, weaker framing has dominated those curricula that market themselves as international, such as the programmes of the IB and Fieldwork Education; it is perhaps unsurprising that this type of curriculum has had wide appeal for the global middle class who populate international schools.

Another common strand across different international curricula has been a focus on international-mindedness (Walker, 2016). This is a concept that deserves critical interrogation, and is the focus of the following section.

A Curriculum for International-Mindedness

If developing international-mindedness is claimed as the distinctive feature of an international curriculum (Walker, 2016), then it is imperative to interrogate the nature of international-mindedness and the relationship between international-mindedness and the social impact of international schooling. Can such international-mindedness be developed in national schools, and how might such an approach differ from a multicultural approach to cultural in a national context? In this section, I begin by attempting to define such international-mindedness. I consider two sets of critiques that have been levelled against international-mindedness: first, the argument that it is an inherently Western concept; and second, the suggestion that international-mindedness is a means for the reproduction of social advantage. I then explore the extent to which there is a tension between a curriculum for global citizenship, of which international-mindedness is seen as a critical component, and a curriculum that fosters national citizenship.

Hill (2012), formerly the Deputy Director General of the IB, traces the evolution of international-mindedness, arguing that this concept lies at the heart of international education. For Hill, international mindedness is twofold; it involves a willingness to lay aside competitive approaches to national self-interest in favour of recognizing the interdependence of nations, and it also involves appreciating cultural diversity. For Hill, knowledge, skills and values all constitute aspects of international-mindedness. For Hill, an international school is one that cultivates international-mindedness, whether it is a state school or traditional international school. Hill argues that the expansion of the IB into state schools has been a democratization of international schooling, so that it no longer only caters to a globally mobile elite.

However, international-mindedness – and the related terms – is a contested concept. Singh and Jing (2013) identify ten concepts related to international-mindedness: common humanity, cosmopolitanism, cultural intelligence, global citizenship, global competence, global mindedness, intercultural understanding, omniculturalism, multiliteracies and world mindedness, peace and development.

In work I have conducted with another group of colleagues, we point out that there are multiple definitions of global competency and over 150 instruments which claim to measure global competency or related concepts (Ledger et al., 2019).

For Gunesch (2007), the term 'cosmopolitanism' is preferable to international-mindedness, in seeking to delineate a philosophy that is loosened from the historical legacy of the term 'international'. Moreover, Gunesch argues that the concept of cosmopolitanism transcends the focus that internationalism inescapably places on the relationship between nation states. By contrast, cosmopolitanism focuses attention on personal identity and personal attributes whereas internationalism has an institutional focus. Hayden (2012) demonstrates that Gunesch's concept of cosmopolitanism has resonance with international schooling. Hayden analyses the mission statements of sixty-seven international schools to measure the extent to which they espouse cosmopolitanism, finding that the schools place an emphasis both on academics and on the development of many cosmopolitan characteristics.

Several commentators have questioned whether international-mindedness, certainly in the form in which it is currently manifested in international school programmes, is a Western concept; much of the literature on this has focused on the IB specifically, although the findings can be applied to international schooling more generally. This is partly because the IB themselves have been willing to question this aspect of their programmes. For the IB, there are three dimensions of international-mindedness: multilingualism, intercultural understanding and global engagement. The IB recognize that their programmes have been predominantly influenced by Western schools of thought, arguing that they 'have grown from a western humanist tradition, [but now] the influence of non-western cultures on all three programmes is becoming increasingly important' (IB, 2008: 2).

In a report commissioned by the IB examining international-mindedness, Singh and Jing (2013) discuss how this Western heritage of the programmes has impacted on how international-mindedness has been conceptualized, and seek to clarify the use of the concept to enable non-Western intellectual thought to influence its future development in IB programmes. Singh and Jing (2013) problematize the dichotomy of Western/non-Western, noting that Western is more than a regional description, but is a mindset that may have been internalized in diverse geographical regions. They note that the assumption that the humanist tradition is a Western one is itself problematic. Singh and Jing (2013) also note that a focus on international-mindedness in an English-medium programme may serve to detach people from their own language, culture and traditions, and to erode local/ national languages. They also suggest that internationally minded service projects have sometimes seemed to rest on stereotypes of the 'other'.

Other researchers have echoed these concerns, identifying a number of ways in which the approaches taken by international schools can remain Western in orientation. Gardner-McTaggart (2019a) studied leaders of IB schools and found that they gave lower status to the IB Learner Profile than to their own Christian values in underpinning their approach to global citizenship education. Ledger (2016) points out the impediments to international-mindedness in the IB schools she studied in rural Indonesia, noting that language and cultural barriers can prevent international school teachers from establishing meaningful connections with the local community and result in only superficial connections being made. Ledger discusses how the schools she studied in rural Indonesia attempted to pop their cultural bubbles and pursue deeper international-mindedness.

The consequence of a Western mindset can be that 'international-mindedness' can become cultural dislocation for non-Western students in international schools. Wright and Buchanan (2017) explore the life histories of people who took IB programmes, looking at both international schools and national schools. For many of their participants, their internationally minded schooling opened up their world view and exposed them to more life possibilities, although some speak of cultural dislocation, struggling to fit back into their own countries and cultures after experiencing an IB education.

The question remains whether international-mindedness can be revised or reconceptualized to incorporate other, non-Western perspectives. For example, Mansilla and Wilson (2020) attempt a reformulation of global competence that integrates both Chinese and non-Chinese educational philosophies. Through working with both Chinese and foreign teachers, they develop a deliberately hybrid conceptualization of four 'virtuous dispositions' that assist students in negotiating an interconnected world. They argue that transnational dialogue is necessary to establishing such shared understandings, and call for the kind of longitudinal, participatory, co-construction of understanding that they undertook for their study.

However, a second, more fundamental, criticism has been levelled at programmes promoting international-mindedness. For some researchers – and I concur – the privileging of certain world views is not an unfortunate side effect but inherent to international schooling. In other words, the concept of global competence or international-mindedness in international schools is a narrative that serves the interests of dominant groups, by legitimating the advantage such students obtain in terms of a seemingly progressive plea for intercultural understanding. Critique of systematic inequalities by social class, language, ethnicity and nationality is occluded by this narrative.

The critique of international-mindedness (or its related concepts) as inherently connected to privilege has been made on several grounds. For some, it is what a focus on international-mindedness ignores that is significant. For example, Singh and Jing (2013) suggest that a concern with international-mindedness may seem a luxury that distracts attention from more pressing needs of ordinary people. Indeed, Bunnell et al. (2020) go so far as to see it as a shared class consciousness that gives the global elite a form of class solidarity. Similarly, a critical reader cannot but see cosmopolitanism as bound to privilege when Gunesch (2007) says that travel is necessary (though not sufficient) for becoming cosmopolitan. In my own work with colleagues, we have demonstrated that the construction of global competency proffered by PISA is one that is only accessible to a privileged elite who travel, host exchange students and eat out to enjoy varied cuisines. It is also an essentially passive construction of competency, whereby students are equipped to cope with a changing world rather than empowered to be the agents of change (Ledger et al., 2019). Savva and Stanfield (2018) argue that discussion of international-mindedness has largely been confined to the IB community or to IB-funded research, and has failed to engage with the wider literature on character education. They argue that many in international schools see international-mindedness as something acquired through osmosis through a long sojourn abroad and an involvement in international education, whereas Savva and Stanfield argue that international-mindedness needs to be developed in a more intentional manner.

More fundamentally, others have argued that the development of international-mindedness is used to perpetuate and legitimate privilege. Although at the individual level it seems to be a desirable character trait, critical analysis has suggested it is a route employed by the global middle class to gain social advantage in a globalized world. One example of an analyst taking this approach is the work of Weenink (2008), although his data was collected from the internationalized stream of a state-funded school in the Netherlands rather than from an international school per se. For Weenink (2008), this type of education is developing 'cosmopolitan capital' in students, the ability to engage confidently and effectively in globalized social arenas. Drawing on interviews and a survey with the parents who had chosen this stream, Weenink concludes that they viewed cosmopolitanism as a form of cultural and social capital. He differentiates between two types of parents, the dedicated cosmopolitans who were advocates of exploring the cosmopolitan world and the pragmatic cosmopolitans, who viewed cosmopolitanism more instrumentally as something needed to function in the contemporary world and largely focused on the language skills involved. Interestingly, Weenink's survey does not find that upper-middle-class parents are more likely to see a need for cosmopolitan capital than parents from less affluent backgrounds; however, what he does find is that parents who are ambitious for their children's future, regardless of their own social position, are more likely to see the need for it.

A number of subsequent researchers have seen the impact of international-mindedness in similar terms, each drawing on Bourdieu's work on social capital in slightly different ways to understand how international-mindedness may contribute to the reproduction of social advantage. For example, Marshall (2011) builds on Weenink's work in her discussion of cosmopolitanism in international schools by identifying the types of knowledge, forms of engagement and practical competencies required for privileged markets. Ledger et al. (2014) examine the view that the IB programmes develop 'global cultural capital'. It should be noted that these critiques do not simply look at international-mindedness, but examine how a focus on international-mindedness combines with other elements of the IB programmes to develop social capital for a globally mobile social elite.

Bolay and Rey (2020) term the subjectivities being constructed by the Swiss international schools they study as 'corporate cosmopolitanism'. They note that the focus of the schools on national diversity ignores other forms of cultural diversity, and that claims to diversity are usually based on the number of nationalities represented in the student population. They note how assumptions about student mobility are woven into lessons and that multiple nationalities are taken as evidence of being a 'true' international school (in contrast to those dominated by host country nationals in parts of Asia). Bolay and Rey (2020) suggest that in such ways mobility itself is reframed as a 'flexible competence' (p. 121), and indeed the school leaders explained to the researchers that they were preparing their students to be freelance workers in globally mobile futures. Bolay and Rey conclude that the cosmopolitan subjectivities constructed during international schooling, in which children 'learn to construct, perform, value and make use of their diversity and mobility' (p. 124) are developing a form of cosmopolitanism needed for the corporate milieu.

This parallels Resnik's (2009) claim that the IB programmes develop skills in students that match the skills and dispositions needed to manage global corporations. Resnik (2009) distinguishes between civic multiculturalism and corporate multiculturalism, with the former focused on building social understanding and the latter focused on managing multiculturalism to glean economic benefits. Through detailed content analysis of the IB Diploma Programme and IB Middle Years Programme, Resnik suggests that there are various ways in which these programmes develop the skills and dispositions needed for corporate multiculturalism. For example, she points to their emphasis on problem-solving, creativity and resourcefulness, as well as their focus on flexibility, adaptability and ability to manage uncertainty, to suggest that these programmes enable their graduates to manage a diverse organization and respond to the needs of diverse clients. Similarly, she analyses the communication skills required by the programmes, suggesting that their emphasis on collaboration and communication skills prepares students to work confidently in multilingual environments and to lead effectively in multicultural contexts. Resnik points to the increasing number of private schools, for example in the UK, who are turning to the IB in place of the national curriculum, as well as state schools in middle-class areas, as wealthy parents seek to secure their child's transition into the global middle class. Resnik argues:

> International and private schools, which educate the children of elite classes, invest effort in developing multicultural individuals by fostering emotional multiculturalism, cognitive multiculturalism and socio-communicative multiculturalism. By contrast, state schools catering to the students of the majority population downplay the role of civic multiculturalism in their curriculum without incorporating new multicultural competencies. As a result, only children graduating from international and exclusive private schools may have access to prestigious global jobs that required multicultural skills; for the rest of the students, even the most brilliant, becoming a global manager might remain only a dream, an impossible mission.
>
> (Resnik, 2009: 218)

In summary, the focus of international schools on developing international-mindedness is simultaneously both encouragement of a progressive characteristic in an individual and also a means to embed social advantage in a globalized world. The ability to interact with diverse others is also required by members of the global precariat (Filipino maids living in the Middle East, for example) as well as the elite, but international school qualifications provide legitimation of the assignment of leadership positions to those in possession of external validation of such skills. This advantage through international-mindedness may not be consciously sought by individuals; Bates (2011b) notes that whilst the IB promote international-mindedness as one of the core elements of their programme, many parents and students select it for its academic rigour, and the hope that it will unlock the door of elite higher education institutions, and have little or no interest in the international-mindedness of the programme. However, there is convincing evidence to suggest that the form in which international-mindedness is manifested in many international schools is both a Westernized concept and a means to replicate the habitus of the globally mobile elite.

The International and the National: An Uneasy Relationship

The focus of some international curricula and many international schools on the development of international-mindedness, and the determination of what constitutes core knowledge, skills and dispositions from outside a country has led many countries historically to restrict the ability of their own nationals to attend international schools (as discussed in Chapter 1). The global citizenship that is purported to be one of the advantages of attending an international school has been assumed to be in conflict with the development of national citizenship. International schools were seen as a threat to national cohesion, national identity and the national language. The expansion of international schooling to host country nationals has necessitated a renegotiation of the uneasy relationship between the national and the international, and the international school curriculum is a contested site in which tensions between the national and the international are played out. There may, for example, be a tension between the values of the international curriculum and national priorities. As a result, we may see both the influence of the national context on the international curriculum and the influence of the international curriculum on its national re-interpretation, with the two in a dialectical relationship.

The expanding use of international programmes in national schools is one example of this phenomenon. In 2020, 3583 schools worldwide ran the IB's Diploma Programme, of which 1612 were state schools (45 per cent). Approximately, 27 per cent of all DP schools were in the United States (with 87 per cent of those schools being state schools). Of the ninety-seven DP schools in the UK, twenty-four were state schools (IB, 2020c). In other words, the IB is no longer simply about international education, but has become intimately involved in the public sector across many countries. The international and the national are increasingly intertwined.

The concerns of the national state have historically had a strong (sometimes, determining) influence on the individual school's curriculum. Green (2019) notes that across much of South-East Asia the concept of a national curriculum would seem alien, because there is no other way of conceptualizing curriculum other than at the national level. By contrast, in some European countries – such as the Netherlands or Switzerland – the curriculum is developed at a more local level. Green points out that a number of national issues have dominated debates about the curriculum, such as national identity, national security, national culture and the national language, and that even when a curriculum is not defined as being 'national', infusion of such concerns into it can mean that it is de facto such (Green, 2019). For Green, even in the age of globalization, curriculum remains 'nationally-inflected' (p. 180). Similarly, Pinar (2010) argues for 'the primacy of the nation in curriculum reform' (p. 2), arguing that the word 'internationalization' is more helpful than 'globalization' because it points to the significance of 'the national context in which global politics is enacted' (p. 2).

Resnik's (2012b) study of IB schools in England, France, Israel, Argentina and Chile demonstrates the dialectic relationship between the national and the international in curriculum development. Her case studies show the international has unintended consequences for national systems of education; she offers examples of teachers adapting their teaching of national curricula, having drawn inspiration from IB programmes, and of national and local policymakers seemingly drawing on IB innovations. Conversely, she argues that the IB's spread into diverse localities has changed its nature, with the IB becoming more rigid and less innovative as it tries to match national needs. Resnik argues that its liberal humanist philosophy, with a focus on international understanding and education of the whole person, has been replaced by a neoliberal approach, geared to the skills and dispositions needed for the global economy and the IB itself trying to match market demands. In other words, the IB is part of the denationalization of curriculum, according to Resnik.

This concern may be particularly strong in countries where the national language is not English. For my current research (Bailey, 2021), I interviewed Bahraini parents using international schools in Bahrain and found that a recurrent concern was their children's level of Arabic, although Arabic was a compulsory subject for all Arabic speakers in Bahrain. The parents discussed the different forms of Arabic used in school and in Bahrain, and were concerned that their children were losing the ability to communicate effectively in national contexts. They doubted whether they would be able to seek employment in the public sector, for example.

Doherty (2009) reaches a similar conclusion, looking at narratives around the IB curriculum in Australia by analysing how the IB curriculum is discussed in newspaper articles, paying attention to the attributes being claimed for the IB itself, for its potential students and for its graduates. Doherty finds that the IB curriculum is presented as an alternative to the state curriculum, as a way for schools to retain aspirational parents who may otherwise move their children elsewhere, and as an academic route to distinction and university entrance for students. Doherty suggests that such texts discourage 'undesirable' students from taking the IB, thereby retaining its brand as a route for high achievers, and it evades any narrative that a curriculum should be locally developed for local needs.

This is not to say that the international turn can simplistically be seen as removing power from national bodies. Steiner-Khamsi and Dugonjić-Rodwin (2018) argue that international private education providers have been used by governments to influence national policy developments in education. They argue that in some settings, IB schools have been officially encouraged as a route to improving national education – either by being integrated into the public sector or by private institutions being used as a focal point for reforming neighbouring public institutions.

This complex relationship between the national and the international means that the international curriculum can, in some contexts, become a contested site for curriculum policy enactment. My study with colleagues of the IB's Middle Years Programme in the UAE exemplifies the tensions that can result.

Example: IB Schools in the United Arab Emirates (UAE)

In our study of MYP schools in the UAE (Stevenson et al., 2017), the IB commissioned us to explore whether there was a tension between the IB and national regulatory frameworks. We found that the private schools we visited operated a dual curriculum system, whereby the MYP was combined with local curriculum requirements. The latter stipulated the Arabic language curriculum, the Islamic Studies and the UAE Social Studies that students must follow. In other words, although many of these were avowedly international schools, the UAE Ministry of Education stipulated that they must pay attention to national requirements in aspects of their curriculum.

Our study noted key differences between the curriculum approach of the IB and the national authorities. The IB allows flexibility for schools to create their own curriculum from their loose programmes, so that these dual systems can operate. In our report to the IB, we noted:

> This flexibility extends to assessment, and the ways in which teachers make judgements about student learning. In the MYP assessment can be seen as the servant of the curriculum, rather than the other way round.
>
> (Stevenson et al., 2017: 90)

By contrast, the UAE curriculum is more tightly prescribed, including externally determined assessments and required resources.

It was clear that our case study schools needed to actively work to construct unity from these dual identities. In other words, these two curriculums were not mechanistically implemented in a school, but were actively interpreted, with schools working hard to ensure that these dual approaches were complementary and conjoined. Our study demonstrated how local contexts impacted on how reconciliation of the two frameworks was achieved, as we contrasted schools in different emirates, although both shared the same national context.

Although we did not discuss this in our report for the IB, it is possible to conceptualize our conclusion that the schools had two curriculum masters by drawing on the work of Bernstein (1975) discussed earlier in this chapter. One way of understanding our original study is to see the two curricula in IB schools in the UAE as following two different codes (Bernstein, 1975). The IB programmes adhere to an integrated code (Cambridge, 2011), although the DP has stronger framing and classification than the other IB programmes.

Example: The primary years programme (PYP) Exhibition in Russia

For our evaluation of the PYP Exhibition (a piece of project-based learning that is the culminating assessment of the IB's Primary Schools Programme), a different research team visited two IB schools in Russia, as well as other schools in contrasting national contexts (Medwell et al., 2017). In Russia, both schools were simultaneously following both the IB Primary Years Programme and the Russian curriculum. In consequence, although the children were ostensibly using English as the medium of instruction for the PYP, in fact classroom instruction was in Russian. In one school, the topic chosen for the class inquiry was 'The Great Patriotic War 1941–5', and within that children conducted research into topics such as 'City Heroes' and 'Military Vehicles in the Great Patriotic War'. In contrast, a school in another country chose 'How human innovation and technology impinges on our world', and within that children conducted research into topics like 'Green Energy' and 'Technology and Health'. In all countries, children were shown how to use the internet for research purposes, but in Russia teachers informed the students that the internet 'was against Russia' and students told the interviewer that it was important to 'check with the old books'. This is a very clear example of how national concerns and priorities were addressed through the PYP curriculum, with the IB's flexibility in choice of topics enabling schools to reconcile the national and the international pressures on their curriculum.

Global Assessments

Although assessment and curriculum are distinct, they are intertwined, and nowhere more so than in international schools. The IB was originally founded as a curriculum to facilitate global mobility (Doherty, 2009). Established to serve the needs of parents working for organizations such as the United Nations, whose careers rested both on global mobility and on their own educational qualifications, the IB's initial remit was to facilitate university entrance for their children. In other words, its original purpose was to provide a recognized university admissions assessment for a global elite with academic aspirations (Doherty, 2009). More recently, the expansion of international schools has largely been driven by the belief that they are able to improve the chance of admission to university, ideally to elite universities worldwide (Bates, 2011b). In other words, the IB developed a focus on curriculum subsequent to its initial attention to assessment.

The notion of international assessment deserves problematization. Although the idea of international assessments comparing school-leavers across very different countries has recently gained acceptance with, for example, of the OECD's Program for International Student Assessment (PISA) since 2000, comparing the performance of fifteen-year-olds in difference countries, the idea of culturally neutral assessment has been widely critiqued (Meyer & Benavot, 2013). Khan (2009) considers international English assessments to be a form of imperialism for their assumption of familiarity with the nuances of certain high-status (and Western) varieties of English communication.

A similar critique can be made of international school assessments, where international assessment organizations are not intergovernmental organizations like the OECD but are culturally located corporations or not-for-profit organizations based in Western countries. The IB originated in Geneva and although it now has offices in The Hague, Cardiff, Washington, DC and Singapore, the majority of its staff are based in the West. Likewise, international A levels and iGCSEs are awarded from the UK. Such international school assessments can be seen as a form of assessment imperialism. In other words, international school assessment displaces the judgement of who is educated from the national context to a usually Western focus. The measure of an educated person is therefore removed from its cultural context and assumed to have universal validity.

This is beset with both conceptual and practical difficulties, which were highlighted by the international assessment crisis of 2020 precipitated by the Covid-19 pandemic. In the spring of 2020, with much of the world in (or about to enter) lockdown, the IB and organizations offering international A levels were adamant that their Summer 2020 examination sessions would continue. Covid-19 had swept across many parts of Asia from January 2020, affecting hundreds of international schools and thousands of international school teachers, who were unable to complete the curriculum and worried about being forced to organize high-stakes examinations in unsafe conditions. Yet, it was only after the pandemic led to widespread school closures in North America and Western Europe that international assessments were significantly reviewed – and with that a relaxation of the pressure on international school teachers to prepare students online for high-stakes exams.

However, the period of uncertainty highlighted a precariousness hitherto unnoticed in international assessments. The decision to cancel exams (Chan, 2020) was a response to the situation in the West, and was unresponsive to the non-Western trajectory of the pandemic. Moreover, whilst each national government put in place procedures to enable progression of their own students to the next stage of education, no one was responsible for progression of international school students seeking to enter higher education in diverse parts of the world.

As a consequence, it could be argued that assessment practices in the summer of 2020 actually disadvantaged the international school elite. With examinations cancelled, it was unclear what diverse universities in different parts of the world would view as an acceptable alternative. After the IB released results in early July, their attempts to use 'contextual' data based on each school's historical performance led to an outcry from parents, students and some national regulators (Jack, 2020). Both international A level organizations and the IB agreed to revise the grades initially awarded. International A levels followed the lead of British awarding bodies to belatedly award teacher-predicted grades in August; however, many IB students were left with grades far adrift of teacher predictions as the

IB continued to use contextual data in their revision. In the IB's final model, coursework grades could be awarded as the student's grade if they were no more than one grade higher than the grade calculated using contextual data (a decision which bizarrely meant that some students would have achieved higher grades if they had done worse in their coursework). As a result, the CEO of the IB Schools and Colleges Association in the UK and Ireland wrote to universities alerting them to the disadvantage faced by IB students in comparison to A level students (IBSCA, 2020). The focus on international-mindedness promised by the IB afforded no comfort to students. In an international crisis, students who were protected by their national governments arguably fared better than students who had sought the advantage of having an international qualification.

Conclusion

This chapter has critically examined the curriculum in international schools. Whilst recognizing that a range of different curricula are used in international schools, it has been argued that there are some common issues of inequality and the relationship between the national and the international that need to be problematized in any account of the international school curriculum. We have examined the extent to which the notion of international-mindedness (or its equivalents), which so many international schools claim to develop, is historically Western (Singh & Jing, 2013) and whether it serves as a way of developing the cultural capital needed for advantage in a globalizing world and how international school qualifications can legitimate social advantage (Resnik, 2009; Ledger et al., 2014; Bolay & Rey, 2020). We have questioned whether this undermines the ability of national governments to use the curriculum to pursue national priorities or whether schools can reconcile the competing demands on their curriculum (Resnik, 2012b; Stevenson et al., 2017). In other words, we have examined the potential tension between different notions of citizenship, with global and national citizenship pulling the curriculum in different directions. Finally, we have questioned the extent to which international school assessments are a form of assessment imperialism (Khan, 2009) and whether the advantage that they offer is immune to international crises. In these multiple ways, we have seen that the question of what children learn in these schools is a site for the examination of power, and for understanding shifting power relations in a globalized world. In Chapter 8, we examine the consequences for a range of social inequalities.

7

Inequalities and International Schools

Introduction

Inequality has featured to varying extents as a theme throughout the preceding chapters, as we looked at who gets to teach in and lead international schools, and the assumptions that underpin the teaching and learning in these schools. In this chapter, the theme of inequality takes centre stage as we consider the relationship between international schools and a range of social inequalities. It identifies ways in which social inequalities may be reflected in, or magnified by, international schooling, examining the impact on parents, teachers and students by synthesizing a range of previous studies. For example, Brown and Lauder (2011) have argued that international schools may serve to reinforce and legitimate the social class advantages of the global elite. Whilst agreeing with this suggestion, I argue that there are additional ways in which international schools may contribute to other social inequalities, such as ethnicity, gender, sexuality and special educational needs.

Conversely, the chapter then considers the opposing view – that international schools can redress or even challenge social inequalities. I argue that in some contexts international schools can offer a safe space for oppressed minorities. In addition, I note that with the rise of host-country nationals attending international schools, they offer a way for the global redistribution of educational capital from developed Western nations to the global South. Again, I look at a range of social inequalities in order to create a nuanced account of the ways in which international schools can inhibit the social reproduction of advantage.

In explaining the complex relationship between international schooling and social inequalities, it is imperative to recognize the heterogeneity of the sector. For example, a socially progressive, idealistic conception of internationalism has led to the establishment of some institutions; others are utilitarian in origin, to obviate the need for young expatriates to travel thousands of miles to boarding schools in their home country; still others are established as for-profit institutions with a market-driven ideology. Furthermore, within each institution different stakeholders may subscribe to different ideologies and tensions may surface as they compete for dominance.

I illustrate these tensions by describing some examples from the schools I have studied describing how different stakeholders offer competing accounts of, and contradictory visions for, their schools. The chapter suggests that, in consequence, the degree to which international schools are seen as contributing to the erosion of inequalities, versus their responsibility for achieving social progress, remains contested.

International Schools and the Replication of Inequality

The first half of this chapter is focused on making the case against international schooling – the myriad ways in which researchers have argued that international schools contribute to reinforcing the position of elites, to legitimating advantage and to reifying the social construction of difference. There have been a wealth of studies arguing this position; to simplify the presentation of this data, I organize this chapter by discussion of different social inequalities, although it should be noted that the arguments within one section often apply to other social inequalities as well.

Social class

If we agree with Bourdieu and Boltanski (1978) that education is a key area for class struggle, then our analysis of international schools and their impact on inequalities must begin with this area. The essential argument that has been propounded by many authors is that international schools serve elites, enable elites to legitimate their class advantage and undermine more egalitarian public systems of schooling. The focus is often, but not always, on asserting that international schools have reinforced the class advantage of the Global Middle Class.

Morrow and Torres (2000) argue that neoliberal globalization has changed the social role of education in the following ways:

1. The rise of a neoliberal ideology of educational provision. Consumerism is expressed through education choice and private providers have increasingly replaced state agents in education.

2. Education used as a means to protect class position. Global inequalities have been accentuated and education has become increasingly important as a means to bolster class advantage.
3. Neoliberal concerns have come to dominate education itself; education for the needs of the global economy is increasingly important. Students are being schooled to become globally mobile workers and they seek qualifications which are globally recognized to support this mobility.

International schooling could be seen as contributing to each of these neoliberal strands by offering an educational choice outside of the state sector: by serving to offer a privileged, high-status curriculum only to an elite and through the focus of many schools on cross-cultural competencies that are needed for a mobile managerial class.

Kim and Mobrand (2019) argue that across Asia, the growth of the international sector, has entailed a 'stealth marketization' of systems of education. They argue that international schools are seen as sitting on the periphery of the education system, so that significant changes – such as the rise of global chains – have been able to occur without much public debate. However, policies across Asia have enabled increasing access by locals to international schools – thereby enabling some (the affluent) to enter the marketized sector but not others. Kim and Mobrand (2019) examine six Asian countries' regulation of international schooling, concluding that state policies have not intentionally undermined public systems of schooling, but have had that unintended effect.

International schools can be distinguished from the elite schools of the colonial era, which sought to emulate English public schools (Kenway et al., 2017). The exporting of English public school socialization through offshore campuses is a recent arrival on the international school scene, and was developed primarily to service local families rather than expatriates who might otherwise ship their offspring back to England. Nevertheless, many international schools are highly expensive, affordable only by the wealthiest sections of society. This does not only apply to schools targeting expatriates; for example, Wettewa and Bagnall (2017) argue that the schools mainly serving host-country nationals in Sri Lanka are only accessible to a wealthy elite. In addition, as we have discussed in previous chapters, they socialize students into the habits and dispositions of the globally advantaged, including the cosmopolitanism needed for globally mobile managerial and executive jobs (Weenink, 2008).

One example of how such class advantage is replicated through international schooling is offered by Song (2013), who argues that education in

English-medium international schools in South Korea has become a strategy for class reproduction by the Korean elite. These institutions were originally set up to serve the needs of foreigners and, exceptionally, the children of Korean families returning after an extended sojourn overseas. Charting how government restrictions on the percentage of Korean students in international schools have been relaxed, and how international school qualifications are now recognized by Korean universities, Song (2013) argues that their composition and social function has changed; nowadays, in effect, wealthy Koreans have been given a special entry route to university through expensive international schooling, one which enables them to evade the 'exam hell' and intensive competitive tutoring that dominates the government school system. They are using their considerable resources to give their children the English language skills that are an entry barrier for many prestigious jobs, and the qualifications that will smooth their entry into high-status universities (Song, 2013).

Some commentators have suggested that international schooling serves a highly privileged 'elite'; others have argued that it meets the interests of the Global Middle Class, which is still elite in many ways but a somewhat broader category. We have met some of these arguments before in previous chapters, but I will briefly reiterate them here. Bates (2011a) argues:

> [A]s a result of globalisation, the growth of the middle class in many developing countries has reached the point where it is now sufficient to support the expansion of such an industry from an elite to a more general status.
> (Bates, 2011a: 1)

International schools are not only creating students who meet the needs of global capital, other commentators have suggested that international school teachers are also being moulded in this way. Poole (2019b) argues that these teachers are developing the Resilience Capital needed to withdraw the precarity of work in a globalized economy. Resilience capital is the ability to take a positive attitude to the experiences of precarity; Poole charts how the teachers reconstruct these experiences as part of a narrative of personal development and opportunities to develop cosmopolitanism.

Ethnicity

Further studies have examined the interplay between socio-economic class advantage and ethnicity/nationality. In previous chapters, we have explored the idea that many international schools are 'Westernizing', but a more detailed exploration of ethnicity is also required, nothing that in many contexts, there is an intersection between class advantage and ethnicity, with class inequalities reinforcing ethnic divides. Before examining the empirical studies of this issue, I introduce the concept of 'whiteness' to understand how ethnic inequality may be reproduced through international schooling.

Gillborn (2005) sees whiteness as fluid and changeable, and as having multiple dimensions, including a refusal to identify with a certain racial group so that discussion of ethnicity is silenced; a reluctance to name racism, instead attributing inequalities to other causes; and a minimization of the historical legacy of racism. He sees whiteness as a performatively subjected identity of which the actors may be unaware. Overall, he defines critical scholarship on whiteness as focusing attention on 'the socially constructed and continually reinforced power of white identification and interests' (pp. 6–7). Gillborn himself employs this kind of analysis to critically appraise education policy in the UK.

This is an approach to understanding racism that equally can be used to examine international schooling. The work of Ayling (2016, 2019) uses the work of Bourdieu to analyse how elite Nigerian parents equate good education with whiteness, firstly at British international schools within Nigeria and, as their children grow older, at (usually British) boarding schools overseas. Ayling's (2016) study of elite education in Nigeria focuses on a group of parents sending their children overseas for study, primarily at British boarding schools. Ayling employs Bourdieu's concept of 'distinction' to analyse these parents' educational choices, arguing that they were seeking a deportment and accent that would serve to distinguish them (and other members of this wealthy elite) from other Nigerians. The children would acquire the recreational interests, the etiquette, the spoken grammar and accent – what parents saw as the 'polish' – of an English gentlewoman/man. Ayling argues that these parents are seeking 'honorary citizenship' in a white world, trying to show that they have measured up to the standards of their colonizer.

Before sending their children overseas, all of these parents had previously used elite British international schools in Nigeria. Ayling (2016) categorizes international schools in Nigeria into two types – with the most expensive (elite) schools seeking to replicate British public schools and the less expensive schools adopting an ethos that is more Nigerian. The more expensive schools (the elite schools) recruit white teachers and white leaders and follow an overseas curriculum leading to overseas examination. Ayling argues that these schools are essentially using whiteness to visually represent their claim to be international; Ayling claims that the valorization of whiteness serves to offer distinction to the alumni of these schools, and that by pursuing this kind of education, these parents reinforce the colonial equation of superiority with the tastes, the morals and the deportment of whiteness.

From a contrasting cultural setting, Tanu's (2017) ethnographic study of students attending international school in Jakarta shows how whiteness is privileged within the school community, with leadership and teaching positions being predominantly given to foreigners, whilst the teaching assistants and support staff are almost invariably Indonesians. She argues that speaking English with the right accent is a marker of status and prerequisite for social inclusion amongst the students. In these ways, being 'international' at this school has in practice come to mean being Western. Consequently, although the school markets itself as promoting cosmopolitan opportunities and cultural diversity, Tanu argues that it has become a site for the reproduction of social inequalities.

We have seen that international schools sometimes seem to be intrinsically Western. In the research colleagues and I conducted into prosocial behaviour, which the IB terms 'Caring', we found that many schools felt that this word came from a Western perspective, and that the term 'Respect' would resonate more closely with Asian values. Deveney's (2005) study of Thai culture in an international school in Thailand shows that while many of the Western teachers were aware of cultural differences and tried to teach sensitively in the light of them, some of these cultural differences were viewed negatively by the teachers, who expected a good student to be a risk-taker who was actively involved in class. Deveney's work demonstrates that international schools may inadvertently expose students from non-Western backgrounds to stereotyping and judgements about their cultures.

A number of other studies have also suggested that, despite a rhetoric of ethnic equality and the valorization of all cultures, international schools may be (inadvertently) reproducing ethnic and cultural advantage. For example, Allan (2002) studied students' views on the cultural dissonance of arriving at an international school in the Netherlands. He found that English-speaking and European students found the school welcoming, but students from other cultural groups, particularly East Asia, experienced the school as strange, Western and sometimes unwelcoming. Similarly, in Wettewa's (2016) study of four international schools serving predominantly host-country nationals in Sri Lanka, parents expressed concerns that these were Western cultural bubbles, causing students to lose their own language and culture. In one student focus group, some argued that girls learnt culturally inappropriate behaviour in international schools that could lead to them being raped or even murdered. International schools were perceived as a school choice that enabled students to learn fluent English and follow an international curriculum – both perceived as useful in the labour market – but these benefits came at a cultural price. A study of an international school in Spain (Codó & Sunyol, 2019) demonstrates how linguistic difference is appropriated by some international schools. The researchers chart how the teaching of Mandarin is instrumentalized to reinforce the elitist image of the school. Chinese was initially justified by the administrators as promoting cognitive skills, but the more recent discourse shifted to distinction – being the only school in the area to offer this curriculum advantage.

The privileging of the Western is not restricted to how student identity is constructed. Several researchers have pointed to inequality by ethnicity and nationality amongst international school teachers. At the turn of the century, Garton (2000) argued that international school parents often want their children to be taught by expatriates, ideally Western-trained and native speakers of English. A few years later, Canterford (2003), in an extensive survey, found that most international school teachers were British or American, with schools claiming to be fulfilling parental preferences for British or American teachers. Canterford argued that employment discrimination takes place in international schools, with these nationalities more likely to be offered employment, and also offered better salaries and employment packages. Canterford complemented his survey data with anecdotal evidence, citing an example of a host-country Head of Science teacher who received half the salary paid to another teacher in the department.

In the years since Garton and Canterford's studies, international schools have become no longer dominated by British and Americans alone; teachers from Ireland, Australia, New Zealand, Canada and South Africa are increasing in numbers (Resnik, 2017). However, ethnic inequalities between international school teachers remain (Bailey, 2015b), and there seems to be an equal privileging of Western school leaders (Gardner-McTaggart, 2018a). In my own study of teachers working in an international school in Malaysia (Bailey, 2015b), participants reported that the division in the staffroom between the local teachers and the expatriate teachers was more marked than divisions amongst the expatriates of various nationalities. Moreover, the discourse of the international educators positioned host-country teachers as having lower skills than the expatriate educators.

Other inequalities

In addition to their impact on socio-economic and ethnic inequalities, international schools may contribute to the reproduction of a range of other inequalities. I group together these inequalities in this section not because I equate them, or wish to marginalize them, but because they have in common the paucity of research exploring the impact of international schools on these other social inequalities.

First, there is some evidence of metro-rural disparities in accessing international schooling. In Dickson, Perry and Ledger's (2017) study of access to IB Programmes in Australia, the authors demonstrate that metro-rural disparities intersect with inequalities in access by social class. They find that most IB schools are located in the wealthier neighbourhoods of large cities. Conversely, Ledger, Vidovich and O'Donoghue (2015) study international schools in remote locations by examining three case-study schools in rural Indonesia. Two of the three schools were located in mining communities; all three were attended by expatriate children, with fees prohibitive for Indonesians. The authors found that the schools had chosen to pursue IB programmes in part as a way of combatting their remoteness, by counteracting the difficulties consequent on the isolation and inaccessibility of these communities. International and localized curriculum policies could be in conflict or could reinforce one another.

Second, there may be gender differences in the impact of international schooling. A psychological study of the attitudes of internationally mobile adolescents towards pursuing an international career (Gemer & Perry, 2000) found significant gender differences; the experience of living abroad seemed particularly important to young women in creating a positive orientation to such a career – although it is unclear whether international schooling or other aspects of the international sojourn were responsible for this effect. International school teacher careers may also be gendered; Sanderson and Whitehead (2016) study promotion opportunities for women working in an international school in Korea and conclude that there are a number of cultural barriers, including gender stereotyping, work-life balance and self-confidence.

Third, it is not clear what impact international schooling has on students with special educational needs. As private institutions, international schools may be disinclined to admit students with SEN (Shaklee, 2007); I have heard anecdotal evidence in Malaysia that some school leaders are reluctant to admit students who may pull down exam success rates. However, this has always been reported to me as a practice by some other, unnamed school leader, and never the school leader to whom I am speaking. This is, then, an area that merits further research.

In summary, there is a growing body of evidence to suggest varied ways in which some international schools may be unintentionally replicating, or exacerbating, social inequalities. The following examples provide some insight into the processes involved.

Example: Bahraini Parents Using International Schools in Bahrain

My own study of Bahraini parents using three international schools in Bahrain showed that many of them felt that the schools were communicating Western values to the students (Bailey, 2021). Whilst they were happy for their children to learn about different cultures, they were concerned about the possible loss of their own values and culture. One parent explained:

> It's nice to be exposed to different nationalities and everything, and learn to adapt to different cultures and all of that. Which is amazing. I mean, they don't have to travel overseas to learn it. They can learn it in this school because it's a small community that has all sorts of different cultures. It's just that sometimes the differences in ethics and values, and we're quite conservative and sometimes my daughter will come and say, my friend is wearing shorts and sleeveless, and I'd like to wear shorts. And you have to explain to her, even though you're in that school, but we are different. But then when the majority's doing it, it's quite a challenge for me as a parent.

One parent acknowledged the potential tension between wanting the Western education that would give access to higher education overseas and wanting to maintain her child's culture: 'I want that education yet I want this culture.' Another parent explicitly rejected any possible attempts to promote gay and lesbian rights at her child's international school:

> We are getting lots of stories about gays and lesbians at schools, and this is again more horrible than *[gender mixing]* to us, you know. It is not acceptable culturally and this is actually forbidden in Islam, so it's worse than having girl/boyfriend relationship.

These parents were clear that they were using international schools for instrumental reasons. They challenged any attempt by the schools to introduce discussion of these social inequalities. In addition, they expressed concern about the impact of these schools on their home culture.

Example: School Leadership in Malaysia

The replication of ethnic inequalities in international schools is illustrated through the study I conducted of international school leaders in Malaysia with my colleague Mark Gibson (Bailey & Gibson, 2019). Several leaders mentioned explicit attempts by the school to manage the ethnic composition of both their student and staffing bodies. For example, one leader explained the ethnic and national composition of her staff:

> I mean Indians we can't help, but other than that we try to make sure that we don't allow for any one particular nationality to take over because, naturally what happens is, they want to speak in their own mother tongue.

Another leader argued that 'international schools want white faces' and described the battle she had had with the school's Board of Governors to challenge this. First, she had to convince them to allow her to recruit non-white teachers 'because they were nervous about the brand'. Second, she challenged the way that the staff was represented on the school website because 'at the beginning, they were just showing the good-looking, young British teachers, the white faces'. She suggested that other international schools deliberately kept the names of non-Western staff and the photos of non-white teachers off their websites:

> Sometimes, they don't even have their photos on the website. They don't mention names. When you go on and look, it's just overwhelming with selling whiteness.

In this particular study (Bailey & Gibson, 2019), we had one non-white leader in our sample, who had stopped wearing a saree to work after the owner of the school said that it might create a barrier between her and some parents. She claimed that other international school principals treated her like an outsider and were surprised that she could understand English:

> The colour of my skin is seen much before I can speak. So, people don't think I have something to give.

Challenging Inequality: An Alternative Account of International Schooling

A more positive account of international schooling can also be offered. In this section, I examine the multiple ways in which international schools may be challenging and eroding social inequalities, or providing safe spaces for those experiencing discrimination in their wider societies.

International schooling for transnational elites was, in some contexts, a rejection of the colonial educational norms that dominated in the pre-war period. For example, when Alice Fairfield-Smith established the Alice Smith School in Kuala Lumpur in 1944, it was still the norm for parents to send their children 'back home' to boarding school from the age of seven or eight. The dangers of war followed in the post-war period by changing views of children and childhood meant that parents were increasingly reluctant to send such young children to another continent for extended periods of time. In other words, the establishment of international schools for the children of expatriate executives and diplomats, the original Type A international school, weakened the process of colonial identity formation. The colonial mentality that knowledge, truth and intelligence came from 'back home' and that the colonized country was inferior was eroded, though not fundamentally challenged, by the growing insight that a Western child did not necessarily have to be educated in their colonial country of origin.

In some ways, international schools are models of equality – the ideal international school is an institution blending children from diverse backgrounds and treating all equally. It brings high-quality education to every corner of the world. It nurtures international-mindedness amongst its students and staff alike. Indeed, in the research studies I have participated in for the IB, I have observed two aspects of inequality that schools were actively seeking to redress – ethnic/racial inequalities and socio-economic/class inequalities. In an Indonesian school that was a case study in the Caring project (Stevenson et al., 2015), the teachers argued that casual racism was endemic in Indonesian society; they drew attention to the ways that their school challenged this, both through their behaviour policies, in which racism was (in the words of one teacher) 'one of the worst things you can do wrong', and also through the learning experiences they exposed students to in the wider community. They expressed the hope that this would sensitize the students to the vast differences in income levels too.

In some contexts, parents enrol their children in international schools as a way to escape from the discrimination that they perceive to dominate their national system of education. Young (2018) argues that

> a new form of international school is emerging in China – one that offers a haven for domestic students from certain competitive and discriminatory features of the Chinese educational system.
>
> (Young, 2018: 159)

Young (2018) critically examines the suggestion that international schools are elitist, arguing that there are two components of this argument. First, international schools are seen as elite because of who they serve; international school students tend to come from wealthy, educated families with cultural capital. Second, international schools are seen as elite because of the motivations that families have for using them; they are chosen as a route to top-ranked universities overseas. However, in her study of a single international school in China, she finds that the families using the school are internal migrants, part of China's newly rich entrepreneurial class; in other words, they were not part of the established social elite with cultural capital to pass on to their children. Drawing on interviews with the students rather than their parents, Young argues that these families did not choose international schools to access elite universities; rather, they sought them out after experiencing discrimination in the regular school system, simply in order to access basic education. Some students had underperformed academically, failed selective exams and therefore felt that their education was at risk in low-status institutions. Others' families had 'household registration issues' – a common problem for internal migrants in China, who are not accepted by every school. In addition, the students at the school were not seeking entry to high-status universities, but were consciously opting out of a highly competitive public system in which children had to cram endlessly for exams.

Another way in which international schools may serve to diminish inequalities is because in some contexts they indirectly benefit public systems of schooling. Resnik (2014) has examined the impact of the introduction of the IB into Ecuadorean government schools. She suggests that prior to this the IB did have a regressive effect, since it sucked quality teachers from public schools to the private sector. However, the introduction of the IB into the public sector has upskilled public sector teachers, and encouraged collaboration between the two sectors, to the benefit of the less-trained and less well-paid public sector teachers.

In addition, international schools may offer a safe space to students who are stigmatized in wider society. For example, LGBTQ students in countries where homosexuality is taboo or even illegal may find that their identity is accepted at international school – although it is hard to collect systematic data on this, given the sensitivity and illegal nature of the subject. One salient exception is Pearson's (2018) doctoral thesis which describes a Gay-Straight Alliance (a student-club to provide a safe space for LGBTQ students) at an international school in Singapore, a country where male homosexual activity is illegal and there is widespread stigma attached to homosexuality, arguing that it offered an important support to students to explore and affirm their identity. It may be speculated that in countries where disability is taboo, international schools can also provide a more supportive environment to children with special educational needs.

Finally, international schooling may be seen as an opportunity for social mobility for international school teachers and their families (Tarc, Mishra Tarc & Wu, 2019). They are often spaces in which educators are highly valued; they are communities in which teachers – a low-status profession in many countries – rub shoulders with executives and diplomats. Situated at the hub of expatriate communities, some international schools offer a vision of a world in which education is seen as the marker of success. In other words, they embody a meritocratic ideal that may not be seen in wider society.

There is, then, a tension in the accounts from international schools. At times, teachers, leaders and students seem to be endorsing a noblesse oblige version of their responsibilities to others (Bailey & Cooker, 2018), which amounts to little more than a giving of alms by these privileged students, reminiscent of the efforts of the heirs of Downton Abbey to take a basket of fruit to a cottage on their estate. In this version of prosocial behaviour, the consequences of social inequality may be slightly ameliorated, but its causes continue unchecked. However, at other times, stakeholders and researchers are in chorus as they argue that some international schools prepare students to challenge these fundamental social inequalities, by equipping them to become agents of change. In this vision for international schooling, it offers a transformative opportunity to influence the children of the powerful.

Example: Teaching Sensitively at an International School in Malaysia

These contradictions and tensions are illustrated by the example of Steve, a British teacher at an international school that mainly served local students in Malaysia. Steve had noticed far greater gender differences in his classes in Malaysia than he was used to (or consciously noticed) in the UK. He believed part of his role was to challenge those differences:

> The boys and the girls are quite different here as well. They are not so different in the UK. The Malay girls I think are much less likely to speak out in class. You have to encourage them, so I've done that.

However, Steve also recognized that his understanding of what constituted gender inequality came from his own cultural norms. He argued that his own preconceptions of the intersection of gender and culture had been challenged by working in this new environment. In other words, he had been sensitized to his own prejudices:

> I think there's a lot of mis-conceptions. I think that when I first came here, honestly, if I'd been on the Tube in London and I'd sat across from someone with a tudong *[hijab]* on, I'd have thought that they were wearing that for reasons about men, not wanting men to see them, and I would not have spoken to them at all. The longer I've been here, the more I've realised they're exactly the same as us; they have the same sense of humour, we joke about the same funny things, and they have the same ideas.

Steve discussed how the schools' staffroom self-segregated by ethnicity. He felt that he had integrated with local staff for a number of reasons, including the fact that he had a visible disability that made 'people talk to you'. However, he was also aware of the potential for misunderstanding – on one occasion, he fell out with a local member of staff. From Steve's initial perspective, the colleague had told a lie, which had felt like a major breach of trust. However, by the time he recounted the story, Steve had come to accept that keeping face was important in Malaysian culture and that consequently things were not necessarily communicated in the same manner as in the West. Steve was concerned that the school didn't do enough to celebrate the students' ethnic identities, saying 'You know, their culture is very important to them. And we almost ignore it, really'.

Steve saw challenging inequality as integral to his role as an international educator. However, he recognized the dangers of cultural imperialism in any challenge he made to perceived inequalities. Steve's position as a cultural outsider both enabled him to identify forms of discrimination but equally rendered him powerless to address it. He felt that the experience of teaching in an international school had forced him to change his own beliefs.

Example: Ethnicity at an International School in Indonesia

This school was a case-study institution in the IB study of Caring (prosocial) learning at IB schools (Stevenson et al., 2015). Ethnicity was mentioned many times throughout our research visit. Ninety per cent of the students were Indonesians of Chinese ethnicity. These Chinese Indonesians are both privileged and discriminated against in Indonesian society. The parents of such students were often highly successful business owners, but the Chinese ethnic minority have experienced historic discrimination and oppression in Indonesia. Less than twenty years earlier, the country had experienced violent riots in which Chinese Indonesians were targeted and many Chinese Indonesian women were raped; afterwards, many left the country. The children at the school typically lived in houses with high walls and barbed wire.

The teacher focus group explained that racism is seen as more acceptable in Indonesian society than it is in Western cultures. They noted that students sometimes saw it as a joke, whereas the school and teachers saw it was a serious issue. They argued that their students could be:

> a bit racist. And probably it is because our students are very homogenous and they come from similar backgrounds and they have been here for years mostly so whenever they have new friends or they make new friends, especially those who come from other schools or other islands, they tend to look at them differently.
>
> (Teacher)

The teachers saw it as their responsibility to make their students aware of their privileged backgrounds. They said some students could be 'affronted' if asked to pick up a piece of paper or push in a chair. Their affluent lifestyle involved at least one nanny per child – occasionally two – and the children were perceived by their teachers as spoilt and selfish. They told anecdotes of children shouting at their maids and drivers, and felt that this behaviour was modelled by the parents. The student focus group concurred that learning to be caring wasn't valued by their society; they claimed that Indonesian people only care about knowledge – one student claimed that applies to 'all Asians'.

The teachers explained the role of the school in addressing this behaviour:

> The kids are very spoilt and quite selfish and they need to have their minds opened and to be less selfish and realise how fortunate they are, and they need to think about consequences of their actions ... It is mainly the result of being brought up by adults who they can basically order around, who spoil them – the nannies and maids and drivers, you know. They are used to having these adult figures who they have power over, ... and as teachers we sometimes need to make it very clear that I am the boss here and you have to listen to what I am saying.
>
> (Teacher)

The teachers also had more ambitious hopes for their students. They described the ways in which they hoped that the IB programme was preparing students to challenge existing society, and claimed, 'They can become an agent of change ... in other communities, hopefully.'

Conclusion: Contradictions and Tensions

International schools both replicate and redress inequalities, both accentuate and challenge difference. There is no simple verdict on the international school movement; it is a heterogeneous educational sector with nuanced and opposing effects. However, it does offer us insight into how complex and contradictory visions for schooling are played out within educational institutions and the ways in which these are interwoven with wider social inequalities.

Tarc and Mishra Tarc (2015) capture these contradictory threads when they chart how international school teachers can find themselves caught in unexpected situations in which they see racism or class discrimination that would unacceptable in their home country. In addition, they may find themselves unable to create the kind of equitable relationships that they would in their own country. International school teachers are brought in to offer cosmopolitan and cultural capital to the local elite, and they end up identifying with that social group; in other words, teachers of international schools occupy a higher social class position than they would in their home country. However, they may remain uncomfortable with that positioning and seek to challenge it through, for example, befriending locals outside of the elite. Tarc and Mishra Tarc observe:

> Middle-class teachers in our study, to different degrees, are attracted and repulsed by an alignment with the elites and, in turn, accept and resist the alignment.
> (Tarc & Mishra Tarc, 2015: 47)

Recent changes in international schooling may increase these tensions rather than remove them. With international schooling now increasingly serving host country nationals rather than expatriate enclaves, how will new stakeholders redefine their purpose? Will this change enable international schools better to serve non-Western communities, or will it serve simply to reinforce socio-economic inequalities within non-Western countries?

As we saw in Chapter 1, international schooling is now big business, but the exact nature of that business remains indeterminate. There is a certain irony that whilst the international school movement was originally established to promote international understanding and cultural awareness, it is now being accused of being a route for the global privileging of whiteness. International schools can't have it both ways; they cannot reject claims of cultural imperialism and still claim to be promoting forms of social equality that sit uneasily with other cultures (such as gender and sexuality). Will international schools remain firmly embedded to Western conceptions of educational rights? To what extent will economic interests trump the principles upon which the international school movement was originally founded? We offer new ways of theorizing the international school sector and look ahead to possible futures for it in our final two chapters.

The contested world of international schooling remains a fertile ground for the theorization and empirical exploration of the reproduction of social advantage.

8

International Education and International Schools: New Theorizations

Introduction

In this chapter, I revert to looking beyond individuals and institutions within schools to the systemic effects of international schooling. In particular, the chapter examines how being 'international' has become a form of control and ascertains the power relations implicit in making claims to 'internationalism'. The discussion in this chapter therefore extends beyond international schooling to examining the impact of the pressure to be 'international' on other aspects of education. It charts the emergence of international comparisons to monitor and control learning, which are now used to compare national systems of education. It draws parallels with the increased internationalization of higher education. In summary, being international is seen as a discourse that positions and privileges, and that both fashions new possibilities and delimits what is seen as twenty-first-century education.

In this chapter, I use a range of theoretical lenses to interpret the growing emphasis on being international. Firstly, I draw on the insights of Foucault (1979) in seeing the power of internationalism as productive and enabling, and not simply repressive and responsive. Being international is a means of constructing the self (Foucault, 1988). Secondly, I draw on the work of Bourdieu (1986) in critically examining the role of language in the definition of 'being international' and argue that the social function of English fluency is integral to the power relations being inscribed upon individuals. Lastly, I suggest that the work of Apple (1996, 2011, 2012) offers a way of conceptualizing international education as cultural politics, and a means for reinventing the international as a driving force for social change.

Globalization and International Schools: Revisited

Back in 2001, Tikly identified three different ways of understanding globalization and its relationship with education (Tikly, 2001). First, the 'hyperglobalist' approach argues that we are entering a brand new age in which global capitalism, global culture and global ways of understanding civil society will dominate. This approach downplays the ongoing important role for the nation state in overseeing education. Second, the 'sceptical' approach posits that we are seeing much more limited change; it argues that the nation state may have an increased role to play in ameliorating the excesses of unfettered capitalism, with education only partially internationalized through mobility of staff and students, and policy borrowing. Third, the transformationalist approach accepts that societies are more interconnected than previously but also identifies contradictory processes; new elites are forming across national boundaries rather than within them, but not all have equal access to the new global rationalities. In other words, globalization is not simply eradicating or exacerbating global equalities but is transforming them. New ethnicities emerge as a result of migration, and new social classes emerge as a result of the shared interests of social classes across nations. Most important for the focus of this book, education has a new role to play in not merely reflecting the social changes of globalization but as a site in which the contradictory pressures of globalization play out in people's lives. Tikly (2001) says of the transformative view:

> What distinguishes this view is the idea that globalisation works both on and through education policy, i.e. that not only is education affected by globalisation but it has also become a principle mechanism by which global forces affect the daily lives of national populations.
>
> (Tikly, 2001: 155)

International schools sit on the cusp of major changes that are taking place in global education. They are in a unique position to critique educational changes powered by sectional ideologies; they are often peopled by idealists, at the very least people who have an openness to other cultures. Their history steeps them in an ethos of acceptance, multiculturalism, valuing of individuals and a mission to help those who are disadvantaged. Historically, they served the families of people who had devoted their careers to diplomacy. Sitting at the centre of expatriate communities, international schools enable us to envision a world in which education is valorized and teachers are accorded high status (Tarc, Mishra Tarc & Wu, 2019). The UK teacher is seen as sitting squarely in the centre of the middle class, accorded status for their education but poorly paid, a fall-back profession in many people's eyes. The international school teacher rubs shoulders with global elites; depending on the school, their children may study alongside diplomats, business executives or even royalty, and many find they are able to save from their salaries, even whilst enjoying multiple annual holidays around the region in which they work. The international school has the potential to pioneer educational innovations and disseminate global best practice in emergent nations.

However, there is a risk that international schools in developing countries may only benefit elites. They may accentuate educational inequalities by developing a cosmopolitan habitus accessible only to the affluent few. They may be seen as neocolonialist, repositioning white privilege as integral to educational success. They may accord power over education policy to the Western oligopolies that are coming to dominate the market for international schooling. They seem increasingly to be serving the needs of international business to have mobile workers, who can build flexible careers around commercial imperatives. Their ethos may be more focused on the drive for qualifications that legitimate social inequalities than on internationalism or cross-cultural understanding. The international school teacher may be little more than the servant of these elites, whose children grow up together whilst each knows their place upstairs or downstairs.

Both stories about international school have been told convincingly before, by their proponents and their detractors. Research data have been presented to support both views. In some international schools, the danger that international schooling reinforces gross inequalities and injustices in impoverished parts of the world seems to be realized. In other international schools, students are being empowered to challenge their countries' positions on the world stage, to power sustainable development and to celebrate their diverse individual identities. At this stage, the metamorphosis of the international school movement remains incomplete; which characteristics will come to dominate are as yet undecided.

In their critical analysis of the impact of globalization on education, Burbules and Torres (2000) argue that in understanding globalization we cannot simply choose between two polar opposites – 'good' globalization that brings higher standards of living, equality, international understanding and justice versus 'bad' globalization that brings Western homogenization, consumerism, commodification and inequalities. Rather, they maintain, globalization is complex and ambiguous, resists easy dichotomies and is continually in tension. I suggest that the international school movement is similarly complex, containing competing forces that are simultaneously both challenging and reinforcing inequality, both driving Westernization and intercultural understanding, both viewing education as a social good and as a tool for shoring up class advantage. It is, in other words, a crucial site of contestation for globalization.

The place of international schooling in evolving social structures is illustrated by the work of Gilbertson (2014), who compares two private schools in Hyderabad (India), one of which serves lower middle-class families whilst the other is an 'international' school that serves the upper middle class. Gilbertson (2014) explains that the first school offers a traditional, knowledge-and-exam-focused form of education whilst the latter offers 'exposure' to different ideas and English fluency. She argues that the rhetoric of social mobility through education is not matched by this empirical study; rather the lower middle-class parents were only able to afford an education that prepared their children for a similar class position to their own, as the cultural capital offered by their school didn't give students the communication skills and confidence necessary to move up the class ladder. Similarly, the upper middle-class parents were not experiencing upwards social mobility but sideways social mobility; the 'exposure' form of international schooling enabled students from recently rural families to move from the rural upper middle class to performance of an urban upper middle-class identity. The focus on 'communication skills' (English fluency, self-confidence and general awareness) were in fact a form of cultural capital not afforded to less affluent students. For Gilbertson (2014), the popularity of international schooling is a reflection of the changing economic position of Hyderabad, with its recently urbanized population and rising prominence in the IT industry. International schooling meets the needs of its newly urbanized elite.

International schools are both a place for the socialization of the global elite and also a key site for resistance to neoliberal approaches to globalization. Understanding international schools in this way also enables us to understand that international schooling may play a very different role in globalization and/or the replication of inequalities in different socio-cultural contexts. The meaning of international schooling in China, for example, is implicated in China's expanding role in the global economy and the move away from a Communist command economy that has motivated the growing Chinese middle class to seek linguistic and cultural capital for their children that enables them to operate on a world stage. By contrast, the widespread use of international curricula in US schools has largely been within the public sector, as part of the marketization of education (Resnik, 2012b). In summary, international schools enable us to examine in microcosm the contested and contradictory nature of globalization itself.

The International Turn in Education

International schools are just one site for 'international' or 'global' pressures to be played out in education. It is important to set their expansion in the context of other increasing moves towards the 'international' at both schooling and higher education level. Cambridge and Thompson (2004) have pointed out that 'international education' is an ambiguous term, used variously to refer to aspects of comparative education or to an ideology of education oriented towards international-mindedness. Writing before recent changes in the international schooling sector, they conflate discussion of international schooling with the latter, ideological approach, although as we have seen recent expansion in the sector has involved a move away from the ideological and towards the commercial. I suggest that 'international education' now has wider meanings; a brief overview of such changes to the 'international' will suffice to explain this view, and to support Auld and Morris's (2019) claim:

> Educational institutions have been among the most active social organisations responding to and facilitating processes associated with globalisation.
> (Auld & Morris, 2019: 677)

In an article focusing on the proposal to introduce an additional international comparison between education systems, measuring their success in fostering students' global competency (OECD, 2016), Auld and Morris (2019) argue that attempts by schools and universities to 'internationalize' their student intakes, staff, curriculum and assessment and research are the primary means by which this response to globalization has been achieved. International schools are, in other words, just one cog in the global turn of education over recent decades. I shall provide a brief overview of a number of other examples by which 'being international' has changed the educational landscape in recent decades.

First, since the 1990s, there has been a marked increase in the number of international students in higher education, which is estimated to reach 8 million by 2025 (Karzunina et al., 2017). Although competing rationales for international student recruitment have been offered by university senior leaders, the dominant justification within UK universities has been in terms of economic competition and the pressures of globalization (Bolsmann & Miller, 2008). There is an emerging body of research into what it means to be international in such contexts, although much of this work has focused on its meaning to Western actors rather than those in developing parts of the world (Evison et al., 2019). By contrast, in the study I conducted with colleagues (Evison et al.,

2019), we examine how contested versions of what it means to be 'international' were played out in their participants' accounts of their professional identities in international higher education (HE) institutions in SE Asia. There were tensions between the institutions' perceptions and their personal perceptions of being 'international'.

The internationalization of higher education has taken various forms. Just as some prestigious Western schools have opened overseas international school campuses, so some Western universities have opened overseas campuses; the UK's University of Nottingham operates campuses in China and Malaysia, for example. Other HE institutions have franchised their programmes to overseas HE providers. Just as the nature of international schooling is contested, so is the meaning of the internationalization of HE. Some see the attempt to internationalize higher education as a move to reposition it as a commodity on sale in a global market (Blackmore, 2004); for others, the internationalization of higher education has the potential to promote cultural understanding and enable access to best practice for all (Hearn et al., 2016).

Second, one of the most high-profile measures to bring the international to the forefront in education has been the OECD's Programme for International Student Assessment (PISA) which compares the achievement of national cohorts of students at age fifteen in maths, science and reading in order to rank the success of national education systems and make policy recommendations. First introduced in 2000, Sellar and Lingard (2014) argue that PISA has progressively increased in scope (of what has measured), in scale (to include more countries and schools) and in explanatory power (efforts to facilitate its take-up by policymakers).

A third international turn in education – one that is linked to the policy development aspect of PISA – is policy-borrowing, whereby education policymakers look beyond their borders for policies that are used elsewhere. As Mohamed and Morris (2019) point out, policy-borrowing can operate in two distinct ways. The first is substantive, whereby nations look internationally in order to identify best practice. The second is symbolic, whereby nations signal reference to a foreign education system that is perceived as effective in order to legitimate a domestic policy (Mohamed & Morris, 2019).

Each of these three global turns in education can be critiqued in terms of the subjectification implicit in the discourse it reflects. Sidhu (2006) uses the work of Foucault (1979) to claim that our common-sense understandings of international education constitute a form of power. Whilst Sidhu's work is focused on universities, we can use its insights to understand international schooling too. People are disciplined into what power-knowledge sees as the legitimate and acceptable ways of being international. When researchers define international schools and question whether Type C schools are 'really' international, they are articulating these common-sense notions of acceptable internationalism. Sidhu observes that the subject involved in international education is constructed through institutional practices, so that the choice to participate in international education is itself an enactment of power:

> Rationales such as individual choice and consumer autonomy that figure in the public discourse, that inform and constitute the utility-maximizing, self-sufficient individualized subject are historically specific and are not by any measure natural or inevitable. In this way, the desire for Western education credentials from the South and East can be related to the broader historical events and geopolitical rationalities.
>
> (Sidhu, 2006: no page number)

In our own research study, my colleagues and I (Ledger et al., 2019) problematized the version of global competency being peddled by the OECD (OECD, 2016), arguing that the model student espoused within this document is problematic:

> The ideal globally competent student has money to donate to charity, has a home in which they can host exchange students, has met people from many countries, and goes to a school which is able to offer exchange programmes. These variables essentially describe the habitus of a global elite, making it hard to see how a child from a lower socio-economic background and/or an attendee of a poorly funded local school could possibly score well on this scale.
>
> (Ledger et al., 2019: 24–5)

Similarly, there is increasing concern in many parts of the world about the phenomenon of policy borrowing, whereby nations take a successful policy developed in an entirely different cultural context and attempt to implement it wholesale in their own setting (Mohamed & Morris, 2019). I suggest that the phenomenon of policy borrowing is encouraged by the subjectification afforded under the 'Global', because if every student aspires to be a global student, then they require the same global best practice to achieve that identity.

Whereas earlier writers, such as Jones (1998), saw globalization and internationalism as contradictory forces and celebrated the potential for democracy and accountability in the latter that they saw as missing in the former, more recent analyses of discourses of internationalism see them as intertwined. Following Allan (2013), I would argue that there are at least two dominant discourses surrounding international education, market-driven multi-internationalism and ideological internationalism. These discourses envelope not only the world of international schooling, but are embedded in how we see education per se.

Being International: The Fourth Wave

The social purpose of public systems of schooling have changed since its inception; Brown (1990) argued that neoliberal policies were issuing in a Third Wave of education, contrasting this to two previous Waves in the socio-historical development of British education. During the first Wave, when mass education systems developed, the role of schools was to prepare workers and citizens to meet the needs of newly industrialized society and to create new social allegiances to the nation state. Mass migration to cities threatened the development of anomie, whereby people felt disconnected from their neighbours and social networks were weakened. Industrialization meant that the skills children acquired in their homes no longer matched the needs of the workplace. Mass education systems were created to meet these two needs. When Durkheim wrote about schools in the early twentieth century, he saw them in these terms; education served an allocative purpose, according to Durkheim – making sure that the people got into the right jobs for them – as well as a socialization role, transmitting shared societal values (Durkheim, 1972).

In the period after the Second World War, however, a Second Wave emerged whereby schooling increasingly was seen not simply as serving society's needs but as a route to transforming society (Brown, 1990). By the 1960s, with the comprehensive school movement, schools were tasked with the job of achieving equitable outcomes. From this point onwards, schools and universities were judged by their success in giving access to the same kinds of education for all social groups; to this day, annual examination results are analysed by gender, ethnicity and social class. Meritocracy remains a modern preoccupation for schools that is far away from the original purposes of mass education.

Brown (1990) identified the Third Wave as the rise of parentocracy; a concern with parent power, parental choice and educational standards which replaced the preoccupation with social transformation that characterized the Second Wave. 'Standards' were identified with the traditional authorities and the reproduction of elite culture of the past. Faith was no longer placed in the ability of the state to oversee education; rather, power was passed to a quasi-market for education and individual freedom to act as an idealized consumer within that market.

I suggest that international schooling constitutes a Fourth Wave in education – the global turn. The 'global' in this Wave operates as a form of subjectification through education. The Fourth Wave is characterized not only by the expansion of international schooling, but also by the internationalization of other sectors of education. Alongside this, the global panopticon includes international testing and comparison of educational systems, the use of certain educational technologies that are supposedly heralding global standards and the rise of international qualifications for judging educational success. The 'global' is a lens by which the individual student, the individual parent and the individual school are exhorted to constantly judge their own performance. 'Global standards' and 'global best practice' silence democratic debates about the purpose, content and evaluation of education, and demote non-quantifiable aims of education. According to the educational philosopher, Gert Biesta, schools and educational systems risk moving from measuring what is valued to valuing what can be measured (Biesta, 2009). The international turn means that we value only what can be measured when ripped from its cultural context.

Whilst the Third Wave was characterized by the language of the market and individualism, the Fourth Wave is characterized by a discourse of international understanding, international opportunities and an opening of education to the world. Whilst there remains a neoliberal strand to the Fourth Wave – I have discussed earlier in this book how multinational corporations own increasing portions of international schooling – the discursive rationality is around what is shared rather than around commercial competition. Resistance to educational reform is harder when the example of Finland or Shanghai or Singapore is used to shame us; try harder, the global turn seems to tell us, and we could be one of the best (even if what it means to be best remains unexamined). Who can question the standard of 'global best practice'? Who would choose their child's schooling to be parochial when it could be 'international', however opaque the concept of being international remains?

This is a form of subjectification that is focused upon the Global Middle Class. We have already seen that the expansion of the middle class in emerging societies is one of the dominant social trends of the early twenty-first century. This is a group that threatens to destabilize the status quo with their raised expectations; no longer preoccupied with the endless job of ensuring survival, the Global Middle Class may raise its glance to critically appraise its leaders and the organization of society. Their appellation as 'global' enforces standards that brook no questions. The onus to seek a global education for their children directs their attention, energy and resources away from elsewhere.

Brown (1990) argued that the Third Wave offered control without responsibility to the state. Some have argued that globalization erodes the power of the nation state. I suggest that this argument should be viewed with caution. I would agree that in many ways the state loses its power; in the case of international schooling, power over the education of citizens is passed to the corporations who own international school chains and to the international organizations that issue qualifications. In many ways, globalization of education equates to the corporatization of education. However, the state is not a monolithic entity and there is also the potential for the global turn to further centralize state control. The local community becomes devalued as parochial; the centralized state seems closer to the 'global' ideal.

Beyond Third Culture Kids?

Let us explore this international subjectification a little further by returning to the concept of Third Culture Kids (Pollock, Van Reken & Pollock, 2010), who are supposedly the unhappy product of traditional international schools. You will recall that these are the children who no longer belong anywhere because of their globally mobile childhoods, which make them into rootless, cultural chameleons.

Globalization leads to a re-problematization of the TCK concept. Fanning and Burns (2017) question whether the concept of the Third Culture Kid continues to apply to children with mobile childhoods. They argue that this concept establishes a binary between 'home' (implicitly Western at least) and the other (the rest of the world). Anything other than a firm return to the 'home' culture is problematized. The term 'kid', coming from the North American lexicon, both re-emphasizes that this is a Western gaze on the world, and – through its pejorative connotations – reduces the sense of agency that may be got through such childhood experiences. Through exploring the experiences of 'Jack' (a student who pursues primary and secondary education in several countries before enrolling in higher education in Australia), they argue that Antipodean society doesn't view identity in terms of the binaries implicit in the TCK concept, nor is Australia located in the global centres of North America or Europe.

The concept of the TCK suggests that a mono-cultural childhood is the norm. In addition, it implies that the TCK will be exposed merely to two cultures – that of home and that of the wider society in which a child lives. It cannot capture the multistaged journeys of many children with mobile childhoods – perhaps with parents from multiple cultures, living in several different places and possibly pursuing higher education in a country with which they have no connection rather than necessarily returning 'home'. The concept of the TCK cannot capture the very different meaning of geographic movement to permanent migrants and to families seeking a temporary sojourn overseas.

In the age of globalization, the types of children attending international schools are changing. Powerful families are sending their children to these institutions, as the rise of host-country national students in Asia testifies. However, it is not just in Asia where international schools are the training ground for the rich and powerful. When Boris Johnson became the Prime Minister of the UK, much was made of his background as a former pupil at Eton College, and the role played by contacts gained there in giving access to the corridors of power. Less attention was given to Johnson's time attending international school, and the fact that Johnson had been a Third Culture Kid (TCK), born in the United States to British parents, moving back and forwards across the Atlantic for most of his early years, before his father landed a job in Brussels. From the age of eight, Johnson spent two years at the European School of Brussels, where he learnt to speak fluent French (Stolton, 2019), before he was sent to England for the classic English elite education of first preparatory school and then Eton College. Although Johnson only attended international school for a short time, it was where he met his ex-wife (Marina Wheeler QC).

The question 'where are you from?' is seen in the literature as damning to TCKs because they cannot give a clear answer (Pollock, Van Reken & Pollock, 2010). However, many people who have had a geographically mobile childhood struggle with it because they simply cannot see the point of the question. To the ambitious child of elite parents, 'where are you going?' is the question that signifies.

Language and Power

Although there are international schools using a medium of instruction other than English, and although the IB has sought to deliver its programmes in other languages, in many places international schools are valued for their promise of delivering English fluency to their students (Mackenzie, 2009; Ng, 2012). ISC Research goes so far as to define international schools in terms of their use of English as a medium of instruction in non-Anglophone countries (ISC Research, 2020d). Empirical studies of international schools suggest that the use of language in these contexts functions as a form of cultural power.

First, the English language serves to differentiate the elite students attending international schools from the wider community. Dunne and Edwards (2010) study service learning by host-country students at two Filipino international schools to conclude:

> English was the language of power because it indicated education and wealth, and provided access to opportunities for increasing both. At both schools, promoting English fluency reinforced the élite status of host-national students in the community.
>
> (Dunne & Edwards, 2010: 30)

Second, linguistic differences may be used to accentuate social differences within international schools. Sears (2012) reports on the experiences of students who are speakers of other languages studying in English-medium international schools. Although the younger students felt welcomed at the school, amongst the older students it was evident that not speaking American English marginalized them socially. Drawing on the work of Bourdieu, Sears argues that some students in the school possess 'linguistic' capital, whilst others do not, which offers access for the former to empowering identity positions.

In other words, such researchers are arguing that English fluency has become a way of asserting Distinction (Bourdieu, 1986). Bourdieu argues that our tastes and our habits of cultural consumption are expressive of class identities, a way of asserting and legitimating social difference. In a globalizing world, English is no longer a means of communication, but has become a form of linguistic capital (Park & Wee, 2013) – that is, a social asset that can be used to reinforce class advantage or facilitate class mobility in unequal societies. We have seen that gaining English fluency is one of the primary reasons parents choose international schools in many settings (Wettewa & Bagnall, 2017), although parents also value other factors as well as English-medium education (Ezra, 2007). Research suggests that in some contexts parents equate good communication skills with the ability to speak English (Gilbertson, 2014).

Looking ahead, it is not clear that English will continue to have this role (Crystal, 2012) – and therefore that international schools will continue to play this part in the reproduction of class advantage. If English becomes ever more widely spoken, it may cease to offer Distinction. Conversely, English hasn't always been the world's most widely spoken language; there is no intrinsic reason why it will continue to hold this position.

What Future for the IB?

We have seen that being 'international' is a discourse that simultaneously promises and erases possibilities. I have argued that it creates forms of subjectification and replicates power inequalities at the same time as it reflects a fundamental revisioning of the social role of education. What, then, do these contradictory pressures mean for the organization that has for so long been seen as the primus inter pares for institutions of international schooling? Tarc (2009) has identified three enduring tensions in the work of the IB. First, there is tension around citizenship, with both national and international aims for education pulling the organization in different directions. Second, there is tension over the curriculum, with a liberal progressive approach to the curriculum competing with a focus on gaining access to top-tier universities. Third, there is an organizational tension, with the transformative ideals that inspired the organization's origins competing with its current reality of serving mainly Western, elite institutions. In resolving these tensions, Tarc exhorts the IB to rediscover the dreams and ideals of its founders. However, other theorists do not share this implicit optimism.

Tate (2013) analyses the ideology of international schooling that is encapsulated in the philosophy of the IB. He suggests that its conception of a universal education that applies across all countries, the pedagogical principles it espouses and the characteristics of the worthy person that its programmes are designed to encourage are all embedded in the philosophy of the Enlightenment. Whilst recognizing that there are many strands to Enlightenment thought, Tate (2013) asserts that they all share certain characteristics: teleology (there is a purpose to human history that can be understood through the use of reason), universalism (there are shared values across all humankind), meliorism (humans can make the world a better place) and egalitarianism (all humans are fundamentally the same and have equal worth). For example, Tate discusses how the IB's Learner Profile – the set of ten characteristics all IB Learners are expected to develop – is a form of universalism. The mission statements of the IB – and of many international schools – are a form of meliorism. Yet, these assumptions about human nature and human history are largely unexamined and taken for granted. With the Enlightenment project being questioned by many thinkers in the age of environmental destruction and the ravages of market capitalism, Tate argues for a greater transparency from the IB about its underpinning ideology and a stronger sense of the IB's contribution to the nation state as well as to supranational ideals.

These competing pressures upon the IB were exemplified in the pressures upon, and its response to, the Covid-19 pandemic. It remains an open question how they will be resolved.

The Covid-19 Pandemic

At the time of writing (2020), the Covid-19 pandemic has had as yet unknown effects on international schooling. International schools have been closed across many parts of the world. On 19 May, ISC Research (2020e) reported on the situation in the main fifty-eight countries hosting international schools. At that stage, only three countries – New Zealand, Switzerland and Vietnam – had opened their schools, although six further countries had partially reopened. Within most countries, however, international schooling had moved online. I shall briefly discuss here the potential impact on international school students, international school teachers, and how international education is conceptualized.

The pandemic is anticipated to have a substantial impact on the global economy; at the time of writing, this remains speculation, but comparisons to both the 2008 economic crisis (*BBC News*, 2020) and the 1929 crash (Inman, 2020) have been made. At the height of the Covid crisis, partial or complete lockdown measures affected approximately 81 per cent of the global workforce, a total of c. 2.7 billion workers (Haak-Saheem, 2020). The longer-term impact is predicted to be immense and economists have started to speculate about consequent restructuring of global supply chains and the adoption of new business operational models (Carlsson-Szlezak, Reeves & Swartz, 2020). Buheji and Ahmed (2020) predict a shrinking middle class in the years after the pandemic, but it is unclear which segments of the middle class will be most affected.

In the short term, this can be expected to have a direct impact on the number of parents able to afford international schooling. Many expatriates have lost their jobs or faced reductions in salary and may struggle to pay international school fees. Host-country nationals may experience economic difficulties too and could more easily move their traditional into national schools; some parents have resented paying exorbitant international school fees when they are only receiving online provision. On the other hand, in locations where government schools have remained closed or have offered limited online provision, international schools may see a surge in demand. International school students may be in the privileged position of receiving the only real education on offer. It is unclear what impact the Covid-19 pandemic will have in the longer term on the aspirations of host-country nationals to use international schooling as a route to university education in the West, for example, whether university study overseas will continue to be seen as such an attractive option to wealthy parents in non-Western countries.

International school educators have been impacted as well as students – their daily lives have been affected and their precarity may be accentuated. Many have found themselves far from their country of origin and suddenly dependent on health care systems of variable quality. In addition, the lifestyle possibilities offered by working in international schools may be radically altered by the pandemic. Taking a job in Thailand or Malaysia may feel attractive when it offers the possibility of exploring South-East Asia during every school holiday; it may feel a lot less attractive when it involves being locked down in a small apartment for several weeks, thousands of miles from family. Furthermore, a job in an international school may be less secure because of the unknown impact on student numbers (Hallahan, 2020). As schooling moved online, parents in many countries started to demand fee reductions (Dhal, 2020; *Japan Times*, 2020); given that schools spend the vast majority of their budget on salaries, meeting these demands would have a direct impact on teachers' jobs. So international school teachers may have increased precarity as a result of Covid-19 (Poole & Bunnell, 2020). Researchers will need to investigate the impact of this unprecedented event on teachers' job choices and on their working lives.

An international event of such magnitude as this pandemic may lead to a reconceptualization of international schooling per se. It is, quite simply, the most globally significant event since the Second World War (Partington & Wearden, 2020) and since the advent of large-scale international schooling. It could have been the moment of triumph for international schooling; instead, it was its nadir. School closures led to a crisis of confidence in the IB amongst international educators. As the virus spread inexorably across Asia throughout January-March, the IB made minor adjustments to coursework submission dates but refused to countenance delaying the May examinations – despite the fact that in many countries school closures left students unable to prepare for, or even sit, these high-stakes exams. It was only after the pandemic overwhelmed Western Europe and North America, and after the UK and United States cancelled their own national/state examinations, that the IB followed suit and cancelled their DP exams on 22 March (Chan, 2020). The IB's failure to respond earlier exposed it to accusations that it gave priority to Western students and to commercial concerns, despite its supposed value of international-mindedness. The idealism that has permeated the IB since its origins, leading to almost-missionary attitudes amongst its educators, may not survive the crisis. Its story hitherto has been one of growth, success and the triumph of international optimism; it is unclear whether it will now experience a peripeteia.

Initial evidence is that the Covid-19 pandemic is exacerbating inequalities (Blundell et al., 2020); access to schooling during the pandemic has been correlated with household income (Bacher-Hicks, Goodman & Mulhern, 2021). International schooling is contributing to this. Whilst public systems of education have struggled to retain access for less advantaged students, most international school students have been able to continue their studies remotely (ISC Research, 2020e). However, we have seen that international schooling was born from a world of interdependency and global exchange; it both replicates and erodes the social inequalities caused by globalization. Although the pandemic heightened people's sense of interdependency, it equally decimated travel. Whilst countries were brought together by the need to fight the virus, inequalities in access to healthcare were highlighted by the crisis. International schooling has been linked to the neoliberal ideology of globalization, but it has also been linked to the ideals of the Enlightenment and social democracy. With many countries embracing exceptional levels of state intervention in the economy, it rapidly became evident that the global economy will have been massively impacted by this global event. Whether the attributes developed by international schooling will be more in demand after this pandemic, or less, is another open question.

We have already seen that the social meaning of education changed after the Second World War (Brown, 1990). As soldiers returned from the front, public sectors across the West changed to create, in Clement Attlee's famous words, 'a home fit for heroes to live in'. It was no longer enough for education to prepare people for their place in society, with occasional social mobility for a talented few; instead, in the post-war era, educationalists became interested in education as a route to social change, and – in the UK – the comprehensive school movement was born to ensure that equity was achieved through education. We have already seen that the social meaning of education has continued to evolve since then, and have argued for a fourth wave in education, the international turn. Yet, the Covid-19 pandemic has already, at the time of writing, radically changed the relationship between the family and education, as parents across the globe are wondering how teachers teach a class of thirty when they can't manage with their own small family. It may either be the impetus for the age of online learning ('Why do we need schools? Look how we managed without them!') or be a transformative moment when people realize the true value of teachers ('Why do we pay such skilled professionals so little?'). Will international schools still be needed once an online education infrastructure has developed which enables a child to follow dance classes in New York and take virtual tours of the

Louvre? Or will this pandemic emphasize our interdependency as a planet and focus all of education on the skills of cross-cultural understanding and multi-lingual communication that international schools have long sought to promote?

This is, in summary, a fascinating time to be a sociologist of education, and specifically of international schooling. I have argued that international schools have been a key site for the contestation of different forms of globalization. Similarly, I predict that international schools will reflect the new forces of the post-Covid-19 economy, and offer a microcosm for understanding this extraordinary social change.

Conclusion: Can International Schools Change Society?

In his 2012 book, Michael Apple asked the titular question, 'Can education change society?', concluding that, yes, it could, but not necessarily for the better. Whilst offering affirmative examples of education being used for personal and social transformation, Apple equally saw a danger in the rise of neoliberalist influences upon education. In that book, Apple was primarily concerned with state systems of schooling, but these competing tendencies towards social progress and regression apply no less to the world of international schooling. He has also demonstrated that alternatives to public schooling, such as home schooling (Apple, 2011), can be analysed in terms of their cultural politics – the ways in which people's 'culture' (including beliefs, values and non-political actions) can lead to certain economic and social realities (normally thought of as the realm of politics). I follow Apple (1996, 2011) in seeing educational decisions – for example, decisions to lead, teach or study in international schools – as a form of cultural politics.

Since Apple was writing, we have seen political changes that have shaken Western societies. On both sides of the Atlantic, there has been a reawakening of demagoguery and a questioning of expertise. Many in the electorate ceased to believe in the establishment, lumping together journalists, politicians, the judiciary and academia as an elite not to be trusted (Davies, 2018). Parallel to such political changes, some in the international schooling sector have turned their face away from educational professionals to embrace decision-making by businessmen with little or no interest in pedagogy or principles. The parents choosing to invest in international schooling continue to believe that education is worth something, but perhaps no more than linguistic advantage in a neoliberal labour market.

As Hayden and Thompson (2013) note in their typology of international schools, there has always been a strong ideological thread to the international school movement – a group of educationalists who hold strong commitments to the promotion of international understanding and global peace. However, we have seen that neoliberal forces have also played an increasing role in the expansion of the international school sector. We are left, therefore, with a similar conclusion to Apple's. Whether international schools are ultimately a force for empowerment, equality and social transformation, or whether they work to exacerbate inequalities, reinforce privilege and concentrate profits in the hands of the privileged has yet to be decided. It is in the hands of all of us stakeholders in international schools – the students, the parents, the teachers, the leaders, the educational researchers who work to understand and improve the sector. International schools are part of the global economy; they are sites for current exploitation and profit-making, as well as being sites for the identity-formation of future elites. Overall, I remain optimistic about our ability as critical thinkers to use research into international schooling and active engagement in the sector to achieve positive social change. This is a sector that has the vigour of the new, that is ever growing in size and significance. This is a world in which the international can be an inspiration to change. It is the responsibility of international school theorists, policymakers, school leaders, teachers and students to capitalize on the potential of globalization and to develop processes and policies that guard against its attendant dangers before it is too late.

Conclusion

Concluding Thoughts

There are two stories to be told about international schools, and two forms of analysis that dominate the research into them. In the first academic narrative, these are institutions devoted to social transformation, exhorting their students to care for others and to engage in service learning with disadvantaged communities. They are staffed by teachers who are committed to developing student international-mindedness. They attempt to respect the local cultures in which they are situated. They no longer simply serve a Western elite, but now school large numbers of host-country nationals in middle- and low-income countries. Moreover, the curricula developed to serve international schools have now been adopted in state schools in many countries, so that international schooling is no longer only accessible to those who can afford exorbitant school fees. According to this story, international schooling is progressive and the international school movement, once the preserve of the Western elite, is democratizing itself. Research into international schooling is assisting this process; researchers have created an expanding body of knowledge advising schools and curriculum developers on how to enhance these aspects of international education. They chart the development of international schooling as a progressive expansion of holistic, idealistic education to increasing numbers of students. This is a story that looks like it will have a happy ending.

However, there is a second story to be told about international schools – and this is the one that has dominated the pages above. According to the second story, the mode of being which is constructed through traditional international schooling – the habits of travel, the character traits encouraged by international-mindedness and service education, the expression of a self which is comfortable with cultural difference through the celebration of diverse festivals – is that of a global elite (Bailey & Cooker, 2018). This global elite – the Global Middle Class (see Chapter 2) – has a shared identity and consciousness nurtured through international schooling (Bunnell, 2020). Admittedly, large numbers of people in the middle class around the world continue to attend nation-oriented, elite institutions, such as the private day schools populated by the London middle class or the former missionary schools that have evolved into prestigious schools in Malaysia, but even in these schools an increased attendance to 'being international' has fostered this shared consciousness in recent years (Brook & Waters, 2015). These days, the affluent in China or Thailand are inducted into the manners and beliefs of a Harrow or a Dulwich campus. They are taught to communicate fluently in high-status variants of British English. They will need to reconcile their national identities with the predominantly Westerns norms of their school (Bailey, 2015a, 2018).

According to this second story, international schools are a cloistered environment and are insulated from the cultures in which they are located. International schools are peopled by distinct sets of educators, both leaders and teachers, whose affinity may be primarily to the international education rather than to other educational aims (Bailey & Cooker, 2019) and have little or no connection to the local culture (see Chapters 3 and 4). International schools follow distinct curricula and forms of assessment that are accorded status in accessing elite higher education universities, but do not promote the national identity or language (Gardner-McTaggart, 2018) (see Chapters 5 and 6). International schools, in myriad ways, create an education apart from that of the general populace, thereby legitimating the advantage that they offer in accessing higher education and well-paid careers. In other words, international schooling perpetuates and legitimates inequalities (see Chapter 7).

In Chapter 7, I explored both of these stories. I considered ways in which international schools may erode some forms of inequality. I argued that some schools in some contexts may be affording access to power to marginalized or excluded groups; these may include people who are marginalized because of their socio-economic position as globalization transforms national economies, but also extends to those who are disempowered because of their gender, sexuality, ethnicity or special educational needs.

However, this book has largely told the second story. This does not mean that the first story is incorrect. Both offer narratives of international schooling that may be true to some extent to some people in some places. In offering a narrative of international schooling, I am not suggesting that this is the only story to be told. What I am saying is that this story is important, and that it enables us to understand important aspects of the relationship between schooling and power.

This book has argued that international schooling both contributes to the reproduction of advantage through the inculcation of the habitus of the Global Middle Class and also provides a fascinating site for the study of global capitalism. The market for international schooling has evolved in ways that mirror broader economic changes, as the glocalized international school (Doherty, 2013) – part of an international brand that conveys elite status, but adapted to suit local culture(s) – comes to dominate the international school market. The rise of host country nationals attending international schools mirrors the rise of the new economies that dominate the world stage, with the UAE, India and China fuelling much of the growth in international schools (ISC Research, 2020e) as their economies rise to prominence. In summary, the role of international schools in securing economic growth and impacting on social inequalities in a globalized world is critical to understanding contemporary global power dynamics.

International schools offer one example of a wider global/international turn in discourses of education. Extending beyond international schools to the internationalization of higher education and the reach for global best practice in national systems of schooling, I have argued that this constitutes a Fourth Wave in the socio-historical development of education (see Chapter 8). It is a form of subjectification that creates, confers and constricts the social positioning of the emerging Global Middle Class.

International Schools in the Pandemic

The second story suggests that study of international schooling continues to be important at a time of global social upheaval. At the time of writing (2020), international schooling is experiencing a year of unprecedented chaos. Outside the world of international schools, Covid-19 has redefined education (Harris & Jones, 2020; Popa, 2020). Teachers are now key workers. School leaders have needed to expand their attention from learning and onto virus control (Reimers & Schleicher, 2020). International school classrooms designed to facilitate collaborative group work and cosy reading spaces have had their soft furnishings ripped out and their desks realigned into rows facing the front to lower infection risks. Some have claimed that the Covid-19 crisis could be a catalyst to move schools away from overloaded curricula and a focus on high-stakes examinations (Hughes, 2020b). The impact of Covid-19 on education will be contested; examining how the elites in international schools redefine their education will provide insight into the emerging world order after Covid-19.

The conceptual lenses used in this book continue to be useful ways of examining international schooling in the wake of the pandemic. In the new normal, globally mobile expatriates may no longer be experiencing the same advantage. In the new normal, the Asian middle class may be facing economic precarity (Buheji & Ahmed, 2020) and the demand for international schooling from host-country nationals may diminish. In the new normal, the Global Middle Class will wish to continue to secure advantage through education, but may have to leverage more limited resources in new ways to achieve this. How will international schools continue to nurture the habitus of the Global Middle Class – now that school trips are cancelled and extracurricular activities are restricted? How will international schools guarantee advantage in accessing elite universities when international examinations may be cancelled? How will global capitalism develop new markets in the wake of this economic shock and what sorts of international schools will develop to serve new global markets? Will the international continue to serve as a form of subjectification when global travel and exchange have been transformed?

The Covid-19 pandemic demonstrates clearly how examination of the international school market, and the social dynamics of international schooling, offers a way to examine global capitalism in microcosm. The importance of the analysis in this book is highlighted by this global crisis.

International Schools in the Future

Any social commentator should be wary of making predictions which can quickly render their work obsolete. Who, back in January 2020, would have predicted that within four months most international schools worldwide would have shut their doors and be operating virtually? Who would have anticipated the lockdowns in the world's major economies, with face-to-face trade interrupted for weeks or months?

So, I am cautious of making predictions, but I can draw attention to issues that will continue to merit attention by future commentators. These will enable researchers to deepen understanding of the main issues raised by this book:

1. How is the relationship between international schooling and new forms of global capitalism evolving? To what extent do these evidence the reification of the Fourth Wave posited above?

2. What new forms of inequality are emerging with the development of the international school market, and do these inequalities reflect or augment existing inequalities within national systems of education?
3. Can international schooling continue to interweave its contradictory impulses, somehow combining neoliberal imperatives with ideological internationalism? Will the entwining of these two either enable the international school movement to strengthen its fabric or cause it to rip apart?
4. Finally, and most importantly, how can researchers influence the development of the international school movement so that its possibilities for progressive social change are realized, rather than its continued contribution to the reinforcement of existing patterns of privilege and exclusion?

In offering us a potential site for finding answers to such questions, there is a growing significance to the academic study of international school.

References

Adams, M. & Fleer, M. (2019), The role of subjectivity for understanding collaborative dialogue and cultural productions of teachers in international schools. In: F. G. Rey, A. M. Martinez & D. M. Goulart (eds), *Subjectivity within Cultural-Historical Approach*, 165–80. Singapore: Springer.

Adly Gamal, M. (2020), Teaching Islam in an international school: A Bourdieusian analysis. *Religions*, 11(7), 338.

Al Farra, S. (2012), Internationalism and the Arab heritage: A practitioner's experience in international schools. In: C. Ellwood (ed), *Learning and Teaching About Islam: Essays in Understanding*, 27–44. Woodbridge, UK: John Catt Educational.

Al Muqarshi, A., Kaparou, M. & Kelly, A. (2020), Managing cultural diversity for collective identity: A case study of an ELT department in Omani higher education. *Educational Management Administration & Leadership*, 1741143220921187, https://journals.sagepub.com/doi/abs/10.1177/1741143220921187.

Allan, M. (2002), Cultural borderlands: A case study of cultural dissonance in an international school. *Journal of Research in International Education*, 1(1), 63–90.

Allan, M. (2003), Frontier crossings: Cultural dissonance, intercultural learning and the multicultural personality. *Journal of research in international education*, 2(1), 83–110.

Allan, M. (2013), Understanding international education through discourse theory: Multinational, international, multicultural or intercultural? In: R. Pearce (ed), *International Education and Schools: Moving beyond the First 40 Years*, 249–65. London: Bloomsbury.

Apple, M.W. (1996), *Cultural Politics and Education*. New York: Teachers College Press.

Apple, M.W. (2011), Rightist education and godly technology: Cultural politics, gender, and the work of home schooling. *Multidisciplinary Journal of Educational Research*, 1(1), 5–33.

Apple, M.W. (2012), Can education change society? In: *Can Education Change Society?* 11–32. New York: Routledge.

Atack, P. (2018), Nord Anglia moves HQ to London. *The PIE News*, 10 October 2018. Available at: https://thepienews.com/news/nord-anglia-moves-hq-to-london/ (accessed 11 February 2020).

Auld, E. & Morris, P. (2019), Science by streetlight and the OECD's measure of global competence: A new yardstick for internationalisation? *Policy Futures in Education*, 17(6), 677–98.

Awang, S., Cheah, K. S. L. & Chua, Y.P. (2020), Challenges and strategies of educational leadership to sustain the International Baccalaureate Diploma Programme (IBDP) in a Malaysian premier public school. *International Online Journal of Educational Leadership*, 3(1), 4–25.

Ayling, P. (2016), 'Eliteness' and elite schooling in contemporary Nigeria. In: C. Maxwell & P. Aggleton (eds), *Elite Education: International Perspectives*, 148–61. London: Routledge.

Ayling, P. (2019), *Distinction, Exclusivity and Whiteness: Elite Nigerian Parents and the International Education Market*. Singapore: Springer.

Azzam, Z. (2019), Dubai's private K-12 education sector: In search of bilingual education. *Journal of Research in International Education*, 18(3), 227–56.

Bacher-Hicks, A., Goodman, J., & Mulhern, C. (2021), Inequality in household adaptation to schooling shocks: Covid-induced online learning engagement in real time. *Journal of Public Economics*, 193 (Jan), 104345.

Badkar, M. (2017), Canadian-led consortium to buy Nord Anglia for $4.3bn. *Financial Times*, 25 April. Available at: https://www.ft.com/content/40cb0d9a-9834-390d-a5ed-287ee3ff48b0 (accessed 11 February 2020).

Bailey, L. (1995), The correspondence principle and the 1988 Education Reform Act. *British Journal of Sociology of Education*, 16(4), 479–94.

Bailey, L. (2000), Listening to teachers talk about their work. In: M.A. Arnott & C.D. Raab (eds), *The Governance of Schooling: Comparative Studies of Devolved Management*, 77–92. London: Routledge.

Bailey, L. (2015a), The experiences of host country nationals in international schools: A case-study from Malaysia. *Journal of Research in International Education*, 14(2), 85–97.

Bailey, L. (2015b), Reskilled and 'running ahead': Teachers in an international school talk about their work. *Journal of Research in International Education*, 14(1), 3–15.

Bailey, L. (2018), Asian or international? Exploring the tensions and opportunities offered by international schools in Asia for local students. In: K. J. Kennedy & J. C.-K. Lee (eds), *Routledge International Handbook of Schools and Schooling in Asia*, 272–9. Abingdon: Routledge.

Bailey, L. & Cooker, L. (2018), Who cares? Pro-social education within the programmes of the International Baccalaureate. *Journal of Research in International Education*, 17(3), 228–39.

Bailey, L. & Cooker, L. (2019), Exploring teacher identity in international schools: Key concepts for research. *Journal of Research in International Education*, 18(2), 125–41.

Bailey, L. & Gibson, M.T. (2019), International school principals: Routes to headship and key challenges of their role. *Educational Management Administration & Leadership*, 48(6), 1007–25.

Bailey, L. (2021, ahead of print), International school teachers: Precarity during the COVID-19 pandemic. *Journal of Global Mobility: The Home of Expatriate Management Research*, 9(1), 31–43.

Bailey, L., Purinton, T., Al-Mahdi, O. & Al Khalifa, H. (2021), Conceptualizing school leadership in the Gulf Cooperation Council (GCC) cultures: Demarcating challenges for research. *Educational Management Administration & Leadership*, 49(1), 93–111.

Bailey, L. 2021. Host-country parent perspectives on international schooling: A study from Bahrain. *Journal of Research in International Schooling*, 20(1), 3–18.

Ball, S. J. (1987), *The Micro-Politics of the School: Towards a theory of school organization*. London: Routledge.
Ball, S. J. (2012), *The Micro-politics of the School: Towards a Theory of School Organization*. Abingdon: Routledge.
Ball, S. J. & Nikita, D. P. (2014), The global middle class and school choice: A cosmopolitan sociology. *Zeitschrift für Erziehungswissenschaft*, 17(3), 81–93.
Barakat, M. & Brooks, J. S. (2016), When globalization causes cultural conflict: Leadership in the context of an Egyptian/American school. *Journal of Cases in Educational Leadership*, 19(4), 3–15.
Bates, R. (2011a), Introduction. In: R. Bates (ed), *Schooling Internationally: Globalisation, Internationalisation and the Future for International Schools*, 1–20. Abingdon: Routledge.
Bates, R. (2011b), Assessment and international schools. In: R. Bates (ed), *Schooling Internationally: Globalisation, Internationalisation and the Future for International Schools*, 148–64. Abingdon: Routledge.
BBC News (2020), Ian Goldin: Coronavirus will hit economy like 2008 crash. *BBC News*, 12 March. Available at: https://www.bbc.co.uk/news/av/business-51851124/ian-goldin-coronavirus-will-hit-economy-like-2008-crash (accessed 30 March 2020).
Benson, J. (2011), An investigation of chief administrator turnover in international schools. *Journal of Research in International Education*, 10(1), 87–103.
Bernstein, B. (1975), *Class, Code and Control, Vol. 3: Towards a Theory of Educational Transmission*. London: Routledge & Kegan Paul.
Biesta, G. (2009), Good education in an age of measurement: On the need to reconnect with the question of purpose in education. *Educational Assessment, Evaluation and Accountability (Formerly: Journal of Personnel Evaluation in Education)*, 21(1), 33–46.
Bittencourt, T. & Willetts, A. (2018), Negotiating the tensions: A critical study of international schools' mission statements. *Globalisation, Societies and Education*, 16(4), 515–25.
Blackmore, J. (2004), 'Quality assurance rather than quality improvement in higher education?' *British Journal of Sociology of Education*, 25(3), 383–94. doi:10.1080/0142569042000217016.
Blackmore, J. (2014), 'Portable personhood': Travelling teachers, changing workscapes and professional identities in International Labour Markets. In: R. Arber et al. (eds), *Mobile Teachers, Teacher Identity and International Schooling*, 141–61. Rotterdam: Sense Publishers.
Blundell, R., Costa Dias, M., Joyce, R. & Xu, X. (2020), COVID-19 and inequalities. *Fiscal Studies*, 41(2), 291–319.
Bolay, M. & Rey, J. (2020), Corporate cosmopolitanism: Making an asset of diversity and mobility at Swiss international schools. *ACME: An International E-Journal for Critical Geographies*, 19(1), 106–30.
Bolsmann, C. & Miller, H. (2008), International student recruitment to universities in England: Discourse, rationales and globalisation. *Globalisation, Societies and Education*, 6(1), 75–88.

Bourdieu, P. (1986), *Distinction. A Social Critique of the Judgement of Taste*. London: Routledge & Kegan Paul.

Bourdieu, P. (1991), *Language and Symbolic Power*. Cambridge, MA: Harvard University Press.

Bourdieu, P. (1998), *The State Nobility: Elite Schools in the Field of Power*. Revised reprint. Stanford, CA: Stanford University Press.

Bourdieu, P. & Boltanski, L. (1978), Changes in social structure and changes in the demand for education. In: S. Giner & M. Archer (eds), *Contemporary Europe: Social Structure*, 197–227. London: Routledge & Kegan Paul.

Bowles, S. & Gintis, H. (1976), *Schooling in Capitalist America: Educational Reform and the Contradictions of American Life*. New York: Basic Books.

Bowles, S. & Gintis, H. (2002), Schooling in capitalist America revisited. *Sociology of Education*, 75(1), 1–18.

Brooks, R. & Waters, J. (2015), The hidden internationalism of elite English schools. *Sociology*, 49(2), 212–28.

Brown, P. (1990), The 'third wave': Education and the ideology of parentocracy. *British Journal of Sociology of Education*, 11(1), 65–86.

Brown, P., Lauder, H., Ashton, D., Yingje, W. & Vincent-Lancrin, S. (2008), Education, globalisation and the future of the knowledge economy. *European Educational Research Journal*, 7(2), 131–56.

Brown, C. & Lauder, H. (2011), The political economy of international schools and social class formation. In: R. Bates (ed), *Schooling Internationally: Globalisation, Internationalisation and the Future for International Schools*, 49–68. Abingdon: Routledge.

Budrow, J. & Tarc, P. (2018), What teacher capacities do international school recruiters look for? *Canadian Journal of Education*, 41(3), 860–9.

Buheji, M. & Ahmed, D. (2020), Retaining a concrete (Middle Class) in post COVID-19 era. *American Journal of Economics*, 10(6), 425–32.

Bunnell, T. (2006), Managing the role stress of public relations practitioners in international schools. *Educational Management Administration & Leadership*, 34(3), 385–409.

Bunnell, T. (2008a), The Yew Chung model of dual culture co-principalship: A unique form of distributed leadership. *International Journal of Leadership in Education*, 11(2), 191–210.

Bunnell, T. (2008b), The exporting and franchising of elite English private schools: The emerging 'second wave'. *Asia Pacific Journal of Education*, 28(4), 383–93.

Bunnell, T. (2010), The international Baccalaureate and a framework for class consciousness: The potential outcomes of a 'class-for-itself'. *Discourse: Studies in the Cultural Politics of Education*, 31(3), 351–62.

Bunnell, T. (2014), *The Changing Landscape of International Schooling: Implications for Theory and Practice*. Abingdon: Routledge.

Bunnell, T. (2016), Teachers in international schools: a global educational 'precariat'? *Globalisation, Societies and Education*, 14(4), 543–59.

Bunnell, T., Fertig, M. & James, C. (2016), What is international about International Schools? An institutional legitimacy perspective. *Oxford Review of Education*, 42(4), 408–23.

Bunnell, T. (2017), Teachers in international schools: A neglected 'middling actor' in expatriation. *Journal of Global Mobility: The Home of Expatriate Management Research*, 5(2), 194–202.

Bunnell, T., Fertig, M. & James, C. (2017), Establishing the legitimacy of a school's claim to be 'International': The provision of an international curriculum as the institutional primary task. *Educational Review*, 69(3), 303–17.

Bunnell, T. (2018), Social media comment on leaders in international schools: The causes of negative comments and the implications for leadership practices. *Peabody Journal of Education*, 93(5), 551–64.

Bunnell, T. (2019), Leadership of 'messy, tense International Schools': The potential scope for a fresh, positive lens of inquiry. *International Journal of Leadership in Education*, 1–13. https://doi.org/10.1080/13603124.2019.1690708

Bunnell, T., Fertig, M. & James, C. (2019), The institutionalisation of schools and the implications for identity of experienced teachers: The case of International Baccalaureate World Schools. *Cambridge Journal of Education*, 50(2), 1–20.

Bunnell, T. (2020), The elite nature of international schooling: A theoretical framework based upon rituals and character formation. *International Studies in Sociology of Education*, 1–21. https://doi.org/10.1080/09620214.2020.1789489

Bunnell, T., Courtois, A. & Donnelly, M. (2020), British elite private schools and their overseas branches: Unexpected actors in the global education industry. *British Journal of Educational Studies*, 1–22. https://doi.org/10.1080/00071005.20 20.1728227

Bunnell, T., Donnelly, M., Lauder, H. & Whewall, S. (2020), International mindedness as a platform for class solidarity. *Compare: A Journal of Comparative and International Education*, 1–17. https://doi.org/10.1080/03057925.2020.1811639

Bunnell, T., Fertig, M., & James, C. (2020), The institutionalisation of schools and the implications for identity of experienced teachers: the case of International Baccalaureate World Schools. *Cambridge Journal of Education*, 50(2), 241–60.

Burbules, N. C. & Torres, C. A. (2000), Globalization and education: An introduction. In: N. C. Burbules & C. A. Torres (eds), *Globalization and Education: Critical Perspectives*, 1–26. London: Routledge.

Burke, L. E. C. A. (2015), Perspectives on British expatriate science teachers in a Caribbean context. *Postcolonial Directions in Education*, 4(1), 53–76.

Burke, L. E. C. A. (2017), Casting a critical eye on the positioning of the Western expatriate teacher. *Journal of Research in International Education*, 16(3), 213–24.

Burr, E.C. (2018), Challenging the monolingual habitus of international school classrooms. *The International Schools Journal*, 37(2), 77–84.

Burrows, M. (2015), The emerging global middle class—so what? *The Washington Quarterly*, 38(1), 7–22.

Caffyn, R. (2010), International schools and micropolitics: Fear, vulnerability and identity in fragmented space. In: R. Bates (ed), *Schooling Internationally: Globalisation, Internationalisation and the Future for International Schools*, 69–92. London: Routledge.

Caffyn, R. (2018), 'The shadows are many …' vampirism in international school leadership: Problems and potential in cultural, political, and Psycho-Social Borderlands. *Peabody Journal of Education*, 93(5), 500–17.

Calnin, G., Waterson, M., Richards, S. & Fisher, D. (2018), Developing leaders for International Baccalaureate world schools. *Journal of Research in International Education*, 17(2), 99–115.

Cambridge, J. & Thompson, J. (2001), A big Mac and a coke? Internationalism and globalisation as contexts for international education. *Unpublished Paper. Centre for Education in an International Context, University of Bath*. Available at: http://citeseerx.ist.psu.edu/viewdoc/download?doi=10.1.1.199.5645&rep=rep1&type=pdf (accessed 21 October 2020).

Cambridge, J. & Thompson, J. (2004), Internationalism and globalization as contexts for international education. *Compare: A Journal of Comparative and International Education*, 34(2), 161–75.

Cambridge, J. (2011), International curriculum. In: R. Bates (ed), *Schooling Internationally: Globalisation, Internationalisation and the Future for International Schools*, 121–47. London: Routledge.

Canterford, G. (2003), Segmented labour markets in international schools. *Journal of Research in International Education*, 2(1), 47–65.

Carlsson-Szlezak, P., Reeves, M. & Swartz, P. (2020), What coronavirus could mean for the global economy. *Harvard Business Review*, 3 (3 March 2020), 1–10.

Chan, H.-H. (2020), Coronavirus: International Baccalaureate cancels May exams, affecting more than 200,000 students worldwide. *South China Morning Post*, 22 March. Available at: https://www.scmp.com/news/hong-kong/education/article/3076349/coronavirus-international-baccalaureate-cancels-may-exams (accessed 30 March 2020).

COBIS (2018), *Teacher Supply in British International Schools: Interim Report*. Available at: https://resources.finalsite.net/images/v1525788139/cobis/cveqgvebqgvjcbrqbcxi/COBISTeacherSupply_InterimReport_web_final.pdf (accessed 20 February 2020).

Codó, E. & Sunyol, A. (2019), 'A plus for our students': The construction of Mandarin Chinese as an elite language in an international school in Barcelona. *Journal of Multilingual and Multicultural Development*, 40(5), 436–52.

Conley, H. (2012), Book review symposium: Guy standing, the precariat: The new dangerous class, reviewed by Hazel Conley. *Work, Employment and Society*, 26(4), 686–8.

Cooker, L., Bailey, L., Stevenson, H. & Joseph, S. (2015), *Social and Emotional Wellbeing in International School Students Aged 3–19*. Paper presented at AARE Conference 2015, Fremantle, Australia, 29 November–3 December.

Cooker, L., Bailey, L., Stevenson, H. & Joseph, S. (2016), Social and emotional well-being in IB world schools: Ages 3–19. Available at: https://ibo.org/contentassets/e2d08ebf9411469088292afc7a5bee8a/research-continuum-social-and-emotional-well-being-in-ib-world-school-final-report.pdf (accessed 22 October 2020).

Courtois, A. (2017), *Elite Schooling and Social Inequality: Privilege and Power in Ireland's Top Private Schools*. London: Palgrave MacMillan.

CIS (2020), Apply for school membership. Available at: https://www.cois.org/for-schools/school-membership (accessed 13 February 2020).

Crystal, D. (2012), *English as a Global Language*. Cambridge: Cambridge University Press.

Davies, W. (2018), Why we stopped trusting elites. *The Guardian*, 29 November. Available at: https://www.theguardian.com/news/2018/nov/29/why-we-stopped-trusting-elites-the-new-populism (accessed 6 April 2020).

De Guzman, M. R. T., Brown, J. & Edwards, C. P. (2018), *Parenting from Afar and the Reconfiguration of Family across Distance*. Oxford: Oxford University Press.

De Silva, M., Woods, O. & Kong, L. (2020), Alternative education spaces and pathways: Insights from an international Christian school in China. *Area*, 1–8. https://doi.org/10.1111/area.12634

Deveney, B. (2005), An investigation into aspects of Thai culture and its impact on Thai students at an international school in Thailand. *Journal of Research in International Education*, 4(2), 153–71.

Dhal, S. (2020), Coronavirus: School, bus fees a huge concern for UAE parents. *Gulf News*, 24 March. Available at: https://gulfnews.com/uae/coronavirus-school-bus-fees-a-huge-concern-for-uae-parents-1.70589865 (accessed 30 March 2020).

Dickson, A., Perry, L.B. & Ledger, S. (2017), How accessible is IB schooling? Evidence from Australia. *Journal of Research in International Education*, 16(1), 65–79.

Dickson, A., Perry, L.B. & Ledger, S. (2018), Impacts of International Baccalaureate programmes on teaching and learning: A review of the literature. *Journal of Research in International Education*, 17(3), 240–61.

DNB (2020), https://www.dnb.com/business-directory/company-profiles.nord_anglia_education_inc.b391b2513740cde758987b560d4a2f4f.html?aka_re=1 (accessed 11 February 2020).

Doherty, C. (2009), The appeal of the International Baccalaureate in Australia's educational market: A curriculum of choice for mobile futures. *Discourse: Studies in the Cultural Politics of Education*, 30(1), 73–89.

Doherty, C. (2013), Making a point of difference: The glocalised ecology of the International Baccalaureate Diploma in Australian schools. *Globalisation, Societies and Education*, 11(3), 379–97.

Dulwich College International (2016), News release: Dulwich College International confirms entry into Myanmar with two Yangon campuses. Available at: http://store.todayir.com/todayirattachment_sg/yomastrategic/attachment/20160427180656179233076_en.pdf (accessed 10 March 2020).

Dulwich College International (2020), *Dulwich International*. Available at: https://www.dulwich.org.uk/about/dulwich-international (accessed 5 February 2020).

Dunne, S. & Edwards, J. (2010), International schools as sites of social change. *Journal of Research in International Education*, 9(1), 24–39.

Durkheim, E. (1972), *Selected Writings* (edited by Anthony Giddens). Cambridge: Cambridge University Press.

Edwards, F. C. E. & Edwards, R. J. (2017), A story of culture and teaching: The complexity of teacher identity formation. *The Curriculum Journal*, 28(2), 190–211.

Emenike, N. W. & Plowright, D. (2017), Third culture indigenous kids: Neo-colonialism and student identities in Nigerian international schools. *Journal of Research in International Education*, 16(1), 3–17.

Everitt, W. (2020), Non-Peruvian teacher attrition in Lima's international school sector: Power, agency and identity. *Management in Education*, 34(2), 50–60.

Evison, J., Bailey, L., Taylor, P. & Tubpun, T. (2019), Professional identities of lecturers in three international universities in Vietnam, Thailand and Malaysia: Multilingual professionals at work. *Compare: A Journal of Comparative and International Education*, 1–19. https://doi.org/10.1080/03057925.2019.1608814

Ezra, R. (2007), Caught between cultures: A study of factors influencing Israeli parents' decisions to enrol their children at an international school. *Journal of Research in International Education*, 6(3), 259–86.

Fail, H., Thompson, J. & Walker, G. (2004), Belonging, identity and third culture kids: Life histories of former international school students. *Journal of Research in International Education*, 3(3), 319–38.

Fanning, S. & Burns, E. (2017), How an antipodean perspective of international schooling challenges third culture kid (TCK) conceptualisation. *Journal of Research in International Education*, 16(2), 147–63.

Fertig, M. & James, C. (2016), The leadership and management of international schools: Very complex matters. In: M. Hayden & J. Thompson (eds), *International Schools: Current Issues and Future Prospects*, 105–27. Didcot: Symposium Books.

Fieldwork Education (2020), Introducing the International Primary Curriculum (IPC). Available at: https://fieldworkeducation.com/curriculums/primary-years (accessed 23 September 2020).

Fimyar, O. (2018), 'We have a window seat': A Bakhtinian analysis of international teachers' identity in Nazarbayev intellectual schools in Kazakhstan. *European Education*, 50(4), 301–19.

Fitzsimons, S. (2019), Students'(Inter) National identities within international schools: A qualitative study. *Journal of Research in International Education*, 18(3), 274–91.

Forbes, J. & Weiner, G. (2014), Gender power in elite schools: Methodological insights from researcher reflexive accounts. *Research Papers in Education*, 29(2), 172–92.

Foucault, M. (1979), Truth and power: An interview with Alessandro Fontano and Pasquale Pasquino. In: M. Foucault, *Michel Foucault: Power/Truth/Strategy*, 29–48. Sydney: Feral Publications.

Foucault, M. (1988), Technologies of the self. In: L. H. Martin, H. Gutman & P. H. Hutton (eds), *Technologies of the Self: A Seminar with Michel Foucault*, 16–49. Cambridge, MA: University of Massachusetts Press.

Frangie, M. (2017), The negotiation of the relationship between home and school in the mind of grade 6 students in an international school in Qatar. *Journal of Research in International Education*, 16(3), 225–35.

Fukuyama, F. (1992), *The End of History and the Last Man*. New York: Simon and Schuster.

Gardner-McTaggart, A. (2016), International elite, or global citizens? Equity, distinction and power: The International Baccalaureate and the rise of the South. *Globalisation, Societies and Education*, 14(1), 1–29.

Gardner-McTaggart, A. (2018a), The promise of advantage: Englishness in IB international schools. *Perspectives: Policy and Practice in Higher Education*, 22(4), 109–14.

Gardner-McTaggart, A. (2018b), International schools: leadership reviewed. *Journal of Research in International Education*, 17(2), 148–63.

Gardner-McTaggart, A. (2019a), International schools' leadership and Christianity. *Globalisation, Societies and Education*, 17(4), 458–73.

Gardner-McTaggart, A. (2019b), Leadership of international schools and the International Baccalaureate learner profile. *Educational Management Administration & Leadership*, 47(5), 766–84.

Garton, B. (2000), Recruitment of teachers for international education. In: M. Hayden & J. J. Thompson (eds), *International Schools and International Education: Improving Teaching, Management and Quality*, 85–95. London: Kogan Page.

Gemer, M. E. & Perry, F. (2000), Gender differences in cultural acceptance and career orientation among internationally mobile and non-internationally mobile adolescents. *School Psychology Review*, 29(2), 267–83.

Gibson, M. T. & Bailey, L. (forthcoming), 'Navigating the blurred lines between principalship and governance in International Schools: Leadership and the locus of ownership control'. *International Journal of Leadership in Education*, https://doi.org/10.1080/13603124.2021.1893387.

Gilbertson, A. (2014), 'Mugging up' versus 'exposure': International schools and social mobility in Hyderabad, India. *Ethnography and Education*, 9(2), 210–23.

Gillborn, D. (2005), Education policy as an act of white supremacy: Whiteness, critical race theory and education reform. *Journal of Education Policy*, 20(4), 485–505.

Goodhart, D. (2017), *The Road to Somewhere: The Populist Revolt and the Future of Politics*. Oxford: Oxford University Press.

GREAT Britain Campaign (2020), Available at: https://www.greatbritaincampaign.com/about (accessed 22 October 2020).

Green, A. (2013), *Education and State Formation: Europe, East Asia and the USA*, 2nd Edition. Basingstoke: Palgrave Macmillan.

Green, B. (2019), Introduction–National curriculum: International perspectives. *Curriculum Perspectives*, 39(2), 179–80.

Grimshaw, T. & Sears, C. (2008), Where am I from? 'Where do I belong?' The negotiation and maintenance of identity by international school students. *Journal of Research in International Education*, 7(3), 259–78.

Gunesch, K. (2007), International education's internationalism: Inspirations from cosmopolitanism. In: M. Hayden, J. Thompson & J. Levy (eds), *The SAGE Handbook of Research in International Education*, 90–100. London: Sage.

Gunesch, K. (2015), Cosmopolitanism and cosmopolitan cultural identity as a model to enrich international education. In: M. Hayden, J. Thompson & J. Levy (eds), *The SAGE Handbook of Research in International Education*, 59–72. London: Sage.

Haak-Saheem, W. (2020), Talent management in Covid-19 crisis: How Dubai manages and sustains its global talent pool. *Asian Business & Management*, 19, 298–301.

Halicioglu, M. L. (2015), Challenges facing teachers new to working in schools overseas. *Journal of Research in International Education*, 14(3), 242–57.

Hallahan, G. (2020), Coronavirus: FAQs for teachers wanting to move jobs. *TES*, 26 March. Available at: https://www.tes.com/news/coronavirus-faqs-teachers-wanting-move-jobs (accessed 30 March 2020).

Hallinger, P. & Lee, M. (2012), A global study of the practice and impact of distributed instructional leadership in International Baccalaureate (IB) schools. *Leadership and Policy in Schools*, 11(4), 477–95.

Hallinger, P. & Leithwood, K. (1998), Unseen forces: The impact of social culture on school leadership. *Peabody Journal of Education*, 73(2), 126–51.

Hammad, W. & Shah, S. (2018), Dissonance between the 'international' and the conservative 'national': Challenges facing school leaders in international schools in Saudi Arabia. *Educational Administration Quarterly*, 54(5), 747–80.

Hardman, O. T. J. (2001), Improving recruitment and retention of quality overseas teachers. In: S. Blandford & M. Shaw (eds), *Managing International Schools*, 123–35. London: Routledge.

Harris, A. & Jones, M. (2020), COVID 19 – School leadership in disruptive times. *School Leadership & Management*, 40(4), 243–7.

Hayden, M. & Thompson, J. J. (2008), *International Schools: Growth and Influence*. Paris: United Nations Educational, Scientific and Cultural Organization.

Hayden, M. (2011), Transnational spaces of education: The growth of the international school sector. *Globalisation, Societies and Education*, 9(2), 211–24.

Hayden, M. J. (2012), Mission statement possible: International schools and cosmopolitanism. *International Education Journal: Comparative Perspectives*, 11(2), 5–26.

Hayden, M. J. & Thompson, J. (2013), International schools: Antecedents, current issues and metaphors for the future. In: R. Pearce (ed), *International Education and Schools: Moving beyond the First 40 Years*, 3–22. London: Bloomsbury.

Hearn, J., Achampong, J., Van't Land, H. & Manners, P. (2016), 'Global innovation networks: The anatomy of change.' In: M. Stiasny & T. Gore (eds), *Going Global: Connecting Cultures, Forging Futures Volume 5*, 206–16. London: British Council and UCL Institute of Education Press.

Hill, I. (2006), Do International Baccalaureate programs internationalise or globalise. *International Education Journal*, 7(1), 98–108.

Hill, I. (2012), Evolution of education for international mindedness. *Journal of Research in International Education*, 11(3), 245–61.

Hofstede, G. (2001). *Culture's Consequences: Comparing Values, Behaviors, Institutions, and Organizations across Nations*. Thousand Oaks, CA: Sage.

Hogg, M. A. (2001), A social identity theory of leadership. *Personality and Social Psychology Review*, 5(3), 184–200.

Hughes, C. (2020a), International schools and global citizenship education. In: A. Akkari & K. Maleq (eds), *Global Citizenship Education: Critical and international perspectives*, 177–90. New York: Springer.

Hughes, C. (2020b), COVID-19 and the opportunity to design a more mindful approach to learning. *Prospects*, 49, 69–72.

IB (2008), *Towards a Continuum of International Education*. The Hague, NL: International Baccalaureate Organisation.

IB (2020a), *Facts and Figures.* Available at: https://www.ibo.org/about-the-ib/facts-and-figures/ (accessed 6 February 2020).

IB (2020b), *Financial Overview.* Available at: https://www.ibo.org/about-the-ib/facts-and-figures/ib-annual-review/year-in-review-2018-2019/financial-overview/ (accessed 6 February 2020).

IB (2020c), *The IB by Country.* Available at: https://www.ibo.org/about-the-ib/the-ib-by-country/ (accessed 22 September 2020).

IBSCA (2020), *IBSCA University Admissions Email.* Available at: http://www.ibsca.org.uk/ibsca-university-admissions-email/ (accessed 12 October 2020).

Igarashi, H. & Saito, H. (2014), Cosmopolitanism as cultural capital: Exploring the intersection of globalization, education and stratification. *Cultural Sociology*, 8(3), 222–39.

Inman, P. (2020), A hundred years on, will there be another Great Depression? *The Guardian*, 21 March. Available at: https://www.theguardian.com/business/2020/mar/21/100-years-on-another-great-depression-coronavirus-fiscal-response (accessed 30 March 2020).

ISC Research (2019a), *China Market Intelligence Report 2018–19.* Available at: https://iscresearchcom.finalsite.com/services/market-intelligence-report/china-mir (accessed 5 February 2020).

ISC Research (2019b), *More Parents Want an International Education for their Child.* Available at: https://www.iscresearch.com/news-and-events/isc-news/isc-news-details/~post/more-parents-want-an-international-education-for-their-child-20190822 (accessed 5 February 2020).

ISC Research (2020a), *Latest ISC Market Data: October 2020*. Available at: https://www.iscresearch.com (accessed 18 October 2020).

ISC Research (2020b), *ISC Research News – September 2020*. Available at: https://www.iscresearch.com/news-and-events/isc-news/isc-news-details/~post/isc-research-news-september-2020-20200916 (accessed 18 October 2020).

ISC Research (2020c), *Data and Intel*. Available at: https://www.iscresearch.com/data (accessed 9 March 2020).

ISC Research (2020d), *Who We Are*. Available at: https://www.iscresearch.com/about-us/who-we-are (accessed 6 April 2020).

ISC Research (2020e), *Coronavirus COVID-19 Update*. Available at: https://www.iscresearch.com/cornavirus-covid-19-update (accessed 1 June 2020).

Jack, A. (2020), International Baccalaureate to revise student grades. *Financial Times*, 17 August. Available at: https://www.ft.com/content/2283fc3d-92a0-4480-bace-7ca3234d7942 (accessed 12 October 2020).

James, C. & Sheppard, P. (2014), The governing of international schools: The implications of ownership and profit motive. *School Leadership & Management*, 34(1), 2–20.

Japan Times (2020), Hong Kong parents want refunds as costly schools shut for months over protests and coronavirus. *Japan Times*, 26 February. Available at: https://www.japantimes.co.jp/news/2020/02/26/asia-pacific/hong-kong-coronavirus-refunds/#.XoGixi2B3Vo (accessed 30 March 2020).

Javadi, V., Bush, T. & Ng, A. (2017), Middle leadership in international schools: Evidence from Malaysia. *School Leadership & Management*, 37(5), 476–99.

Jin, L. & Cortazzi, M. (2006), Changing practices in Chinese cultures of learning. *Language, Culture and Curriculum*, 19(1), 5–20.

Jones, P. W. (1998), Globalisation and internationalism: Democratic prospects for world education. *Comparative Education*, 34(2), 143–55.

Joslin, P. (2002), Teacher relocation: Reflections in the context of international schools. *Journal of Research in International Education*, 1(1), 33–62.

Karzunina, D., West, J., Moran, J. & Philippou, G. (2017), 'Student mobility and demographic changes.' London: QS Quacquarelli. http://info.qs.com/rs/335-VIN-535/images/Student-Mobility-Demographic-Changes.pdf

Kaufmann, V., Bergman, M. M. & Joye, D. (2004), Motility: Mobility as capital. *International Journal of Urban and Regional Research*, 28(4), 745–56.

Keeling, A. (2012), Prospecting for gold. *British International Schools Magazine*, 1, 6–7.

Keller, D. (2015), Leadership of international schools: Understanding and managing dualities. *Educational Management Administration & Leadership*, 43(6), 900–17.

Kendall, G., Woodward, I. & Skrbis, Z. (2009), *The Sociology of Cosmopolitanism: Globalization, Identity, Culture and Government*. New York: Springer.

Kenway, J. & Fahey, J. (2009), *Globalizing the Research Imagination*. London: Routledge.

Kenway, J., Fahey, J., Epstein, D., Koh, A., McCarthy, C. & Rizvi, F. (2017), *Class Choreographies: Elite Schools and Globalization*. New York: Springer.

Kenway, J. & Koh, A. (2013), The elite school as 'cognitive machine' and 'social paradise': Developing transnational capitals for the national 'field of power'. *Journal of Sociology*, 49(2–3), 272–90.

Khalil, L. & Kelly, A. (2020), The practice of choice-making: Applying Bourdieu to the field of international schooling. *Journal of Research in International Education*, 19(2), 137–54.

Khan, S. Z. (2009), Imperialism of international tests: An EIL perspective. In: F. Sharifian (ed), *English as an International Language: Perspectives and Pedagogical Issues*, 190–205. Bristol: Multilingual Matters.

Kim, H. (2019), *How Global Capital is Remaking International Education: The Emergence of Transnational Education Corporations*. New York: Springer.

Kim, H. & Mobrand, E. (2019), Stealth marketisation: How international school policy is quietly challenging education systems in Asia. *Globalisation, Societies and Education*, 17(3), 310–23.

Koo, H. (2016), The global middle class: How is it made, what does it represent? *Globalizations*, 13(4), 440–53.

Lai, C., Li, Z. & Gong, Y. (2016), Teacher agency and professional learning in cross-cultural teaching contexts: Accounts of Chinese teachers from international schools in Hong Kong. *Teaching and Teacher Education*, 54, 12–21.

Langford, M. (2012), Global nomads, third culture kids and international schools. *International Education, Principles and Practice*, 18(2), 28–43.

Ledger, S. (2016), Breaking through the cultural bubble: International schools engaging at the local level. *The International Schools Journal*, 36(1), 27–39.

Ledger, S., Vidovich, L. & O'Donoghue, T. (2014), *Global to Local Curriculum Policy Processes: The Enactment of the International Baccalaureate in Remote International Schools*, Vol. 4. New York: Springer.

Ledger, S., Vidovich, L. & O'Donoghue, T. (2015), International and remote schooling: Global to local curriculum policy dynamics in Indonesia. *The Asia-Pacific Education Researcher*, 24(4), 695–703.

Ledger, S., Thier, M., Bailey, L. & Pitts, C. (2019), OECD's approach to measuring global competency: Powerful voices shaping education. *Teachers College Record*, 121(8), 1–40.

Lee, M., Hallinger, P. & Walker, A. (2012), Leadership challenges in international schools in the Asia Pacific region: Evidence from programme implementation of the International Baccalaureate. *International Journal of Leadership in Education*, 15(3), 289–310.

Lee, M. & Wright, E. (2016), Moving from elite international schools to the world's elite universities. *International Journal of Comparative Education and Development*, 18(2), 120–36.

Li, J. (2005), Mind or virtue: Western and Chinese beliefs about learning. *Current Directions in Psychological Science*, 14(4), 190–4.

Loh, C. E. (2016), Elite schoolboys becoming global citizens: Examining the practice of habitus. In: A. Koh & J. Kenway (eds), *Elite Schools: Multiple Geographies of Privilege*, 82–98. New York: Routledge.

Lowe, J. (2000), International examinations: The new credentialism and reproduction of advantage in a globalizing world. *Assessment in Education: Principles, Policy and Practice*, 7(3), 363–77.

MacDonald, J. (2009), Balancing priorities and measuring success: A triple bottom line framework for international school leaders. *Journal of Research in International Education*, 8(1), 81–98.

Machin, D. (2014), Professional educator or professional manager? The contested role of the for-profit international school Principal. *Journal of Research in International Education*, 13(1), 19–29.

MacKenzie, P. (2009), The attraction of international schools for Japanese parents living in Japan. *Journal of Research in International Education*, 8(3), 326–48.

Mancuso, S.V., Roberts, L. & White, G. P. (2010), Teacher retention in international schools: The key role of school leadership. *Journal of Research in International Education*, 9(3), 306–23.

Mansilla, V. B. & Wilson, D. (2020), What is global competence, and what might it look like in Chinese schools? *Journal of Research in International Education*, 19(1), 3–22.

Marshall, H. (2011), Education for global citizenship: Reflecting upon the instrumentalist agendas at play. In: R. Bates (ed), *Schooling Internationally: Globalisation, Internationalisation and the Future for International Schools*, 182–200. London: Routledge.

Medwell, J., Cooker, L., Bailey, L. & Winchip, E. (2017), The impact of the PYP exhibition on the development of international mindedness, critical thinking and attributes of the IB learner profile. *The International Baccalaureate*. Available at: https://ibo.org/globalassets/publications/ib-research/pyp/pyp-exhibition-final-report-en.pdf (accessed 12 October 2020).

Meyer, H. D. & Benavot, A. (eds) (2013), *PISA, Power, and Policy: The Emergence of Global Educational Governance*. Didcot: Symposium Books Ltd.

Mohamed, M. & Morris, P. (2019), Buying, selling and outsourcing educational reform: The global education industry and 'policy borrowing' in the Gulf. *Compare: A Journal of Comparative and International Education*, 1–21. https://doi.org/10.1080/03057925.2019.1607255

Moret, J. (2017), Mobility capital: Somali migrants' trajectories of (im)mobilities and the negotiation of social inequalities across borders. *Geoforum*, 1–18. Available at: http://doc.rero.ch/record/306080/files/Moret_Jo_lle_Mobility_Capita_Somali_migrant_s_trajectories_GEOFORUM.pdf

Morgan, W. J., Sives, A. & Appleton, S. (2006), *Teacher Mobility, 'Brain Drain', Labour Markets and Educational Resources in the Commonwealth*. London: Department for International Development.

Morrow, R. A. & Torres, C. A. (2000), The state, globalization, and educational policy. In: N. C. Burbules & C. A. Torres. *Globalization and Education: Critical Perspectives*, 27–56. London: Taylor and Francis.

Murakami-Ramalho, E. & Benham, M. (2010), Around the fishing net: Leadership dynamics for change in an American international school. *Educational Management Administration & Leadership*, 38(5), 625–43.

Newman, A., Hoechner, H. & Sancho, D. (2020), Constructions of the 'educated person' in the context of mobility, migration and globalisation. *Globalisation, Societies and Education*, 18(3), 233–49.

Ng, V. (2012), The decision to send local children to international schools in Hong Kong: Local parents' perspectives. *Asia Pacific Education Review*, 13(1), 121–36.

Niemann, D., Martens, K. & Teltemann, J. (2017), PISA and its consequences: Shaping education policies through international comparisons. *European Journal of Education*, 52(2), 175–83.

Nord Anglia Education (2020), Nord Anglia moves HQ to London. Available at: https://thepienews.com/news/nord-anglia-moves-hq-to-london/ (accessed 11 February 2020).

OECD (2016), Global competency for an inclusive world: Programme for the International Student Assessment. Paris: OECD. Available at: https://www.oecd.org/pisa/aboutpisa/Global-competency-for-an-inclusive-world.pdf (accessed 27 July 2020).

Olivier, J., Thoenig, M. & Verdier, T. (2008), Globalization and the dynamics of cultural identity. *Journal of international Economics*, 76(2), 356–70.

Olssen, M. (2004), Neoliberalism, globalisation, democracy: Challenges for education. *Globalisation, Societies and Education*, 2(2), 231–75.

Park, J. S. Y. & Wee, L. (2013), *Markets of English: Linguistic Capital and Language Policy in a Globalizing World*. London: Routledge.

Parker, J. (2009), Burgeoning Bourgeoisie. *The Economist*, 14 February. Available at: https://www.economist.com/special-report/2009/02/14/burgeoning-bourgeoisie (accessed 6 February 2020).

Partington, R. & Wearden, G. (2020), Complacency to chaos: How Covid-19 sent the world's markets into freefall. *The Guardian*, 28 March. Available at: https://www.theguardian.com/business/2020/mar/28/how-coronavirus-sent-global-markets-into-freefall (accessed 30 March 2020).

Pearson, R. F. (2018), *Gay Straight Alliances: A Case Study of Member Perceptions of Support at an International School* (Doctoral dissertation, University of Southern California).

Pinar, W. (ed) (2010), *Curriculum Studies in South Africa: Intellectual Histories and Present Circumstances*. New York: Springer.

Pollock, D. C., Van Reken, R. E. & Pollock, M. V. (2010), *Third Culture Kids: The Experience of Growing Up Among Worlds: The Original, Classic Book on TCKs*. London: Hachette UK.

Poole, A. (2018), ' We are a Chinese school': Constructing school identity from the lived experiences of expatriate and Chinese teaching faculty in a Type C international school in Shanghai, China. *International Journal of Progressive Education*, 14(1), 105–21.

Poole, A. (2019a), International education teachers' experiences as an educational precariat in China. *Journal of Research in International Education*, 18(1), 60–76.

Poole, A. (2019b), Internationalised school teachers' experiences of precarity as part of the global middle class in China: Towards resilience capital. *The Asia-Pacific Education Researcher*, 29(3), 227–35.

Poole, A. (2020a), Decoupling Chinese internationalised schools from normative constructions of the international school. *Compare: A Journal of Comparative and International Education*, 50(3), 447–54.

Poole, A. (2020b), Constructing international school teacher identity from lived experience: A fresh conceptual framework. *Journal of Research in International Education*, 19(2), 155–171. https://doi.org/10.1177%2F1475240920954044

Poole, A. & Bunnell, T. (2020), Developing the notion of teaching in 'International Schools' as precarious: Towards a more nuanced approach based upon 'transition capital'. *Globalisation, Societies and Education*, 1–11. https://doi.org/10.1080/14767724.2020.1816924

Popa, S. (2020), Reflections on COVID-19 and the future of education and learning. *Prospects*, 49, 1–6.

Reimers, F. M. & Schleicher, A. (2020), *A Framework to Guide an Education Response to the COVID-19 Pandemic of 2020*. OECD. Available at: https://globaled.gse.harvard.edu/files/geii/files/framework_guide_v2.pdf (accessed 30 October 2020).

Resnik, J. (2008), The construction of the global worker through international education. In: J. Resnik (ed), *The Production of Educational Knowledge in the Global Era*, 147–67. Rotterdam: Sense Publishers.

Resnik, J. (2009), Multicultural education–good for business but not for the state? The IB curriculum and global capitalism. *British Journal of Educational Studies*, 57(3), 217–44.

Resnik, J. (2012a), Sociology of international education–an emerging field of research. *International Studies in Sociology of Education*, 22(4), 291–310.

Resnik, J. (2012b), The denationalization of education and the expansion of the International Baccalaureate. *Comparative Education Review*, 56(2), 248–69.

Resnik, J. (2014), Who gets the best teachers? The incorporation of the IB Program into public high schools and its impact on the teacher labour market in Ecuador. In: R. Arber, J. Blackmore & A. Vongalis-Macrow (eds), *Mobile Teachers, Teacher Identity and International Schooling*, 95–120. New York: Springer.

Resnik, J. (2017), The internationalization of schooling: Implications for teachers. In: K. Bickmore, R. Hayhoe, C. Manion, K. Mundy & R. Read (eds), *Comparative and International Education: Issues for Teachers*, 335–62. Toronto: Canadian Scholars' Press.

Rey, J., Bolay, M. & Gez, Y. N. (2020), Precarious privilege: Personal debt, lifestyle aspirations and mobility among international school teachers. *Globalisation, Societies and Education*, 18(4), 361–73.

Rockstuhl, T., Seiler, S., Ang, S., Van Dyne, L. & Annen, H. (2011), Beyond general intelligence (IQ) and emotional intelligence (EQ): The role of cultural intelligence

(CQ) on cross-border leadership effectiveness in a globalized world. *Journal of Social Issues*, 67(4), 825–40.

Roskell, D. (2013), Cross-cultural transition: International teachers' experience of 'culture shock'. *Journal of Research in International Education*, 12(2), 155–72.

Roudometof, V. (2016a), *Glocalization: A Critical Introduction*. London: Routledge.

Roudometof, V. (2016b), Theorizing glocalization: Three interpretations1. *European Journal of Social Theory*, 19(3), 391–408.

Sanderson, R. E. & Whitehead, S. (2016), The gendered international school: Barriers to women managers' progression. *Education & Training*, 58(3), 328–38.

Savva, M. (2013), International schools as gateways to the intercultural development of North-American teachers. *Journal of Research in International Education*, 12(3), 214–27.

Savva, M. & Stanfield, D. (2018), International-mindedness: Deviations, incongruities and other challenges facing the concept. *Journal of Research in International Education*, 17(2), 179–93.

Scandura, T. & Dorfman, P. (2004), Leadership research in an international and cross-cultural context. *The Leadership Quarterly*, 15(2), 277–307.

Schumann, C. (2018), Cosmopolitanism and globalization in education. In: P. Smeyers (ed), *International Handbook of Philosophy of Education*, 821–31. New York: Springer.

Sears, C. (2012), Negotiating identity in English-medium settings: Agency, resistance and appropriation among speakers of other languages in an international school. *Journal of Research in International Education*, 11(2), 117–36.

Sellar, S. & Lingard, B. (2014), The OECD and the expansion of PISA: New global modes of governance in education. *British Educational Research Journal*, 40(6), 917–36.

Shaklee, B. D. (2007), Focus on international schools: Serving students with learning disabilities. In: T. E. Scruggs & M. A. Mastropieri (eds), *International Perspectives (Advances in Learning and Behavioral Disabilities, Vol. 20)*, 265–83. Bingley: Emerald Group Publishing Ltd.

Sidhu, R. K. (2006), *Universities and Globalization: To Market, to Market*. London: Routledge.

Singh. M. & Jing, Q. (2013), *21st Century International Mindedness: Anexploratory Study of its Conceptualisation and Assessment: IB Research Paper*. Sydney: University of Western Sydney. Available at: https://researchdirect.westernsydney.edu.au/islandora/object/uws:22668/datastream/PDF/view (accessed 30 October 2020).

Slough-Kuss, Y. (2014), Cultural diversity among heads of international schools: Potential implications for international education. *Journal of Research in International Education*, 13(3), 218–34.

Song, J. J. (2013), For whom the bell tolls: Globalisation, social class and South Korea's international schools. *Globalisation, Societies and Education*, 11(1), 136–59.

Spencer, D. A. (2012), Book review symposium: Guy standing, the precariat: The new dangerous class, reviewed by David Spencer. *Work, Employment and Society*, 26(4), 688–9.

Standing, G. (2011), *The Precariat: the New Dangerous Class*. London, New York: Bloomsbury Academic.

Steffens, N. K., Haslam, S. A., Reicher, S. D., Platow, M. J., Fransen, K., Yang, J., ... & Boen, F. (2014), Leadership as social identity management: Introducing the Identity Leadership Inventory (ILI) to assess and validate a four-dimensional model. *The Leadership Quarterly*, 25(5), 1001–24.

Steiner-Khamsi, G. & Dugonjić-Rodwin, L. (2018), Transnational accreditation for public schools: IB, PISA and other public–private partnerships. *Journal of Curriculum Studies*, 50(5), 595–607.

Stevenson, H., Joseph, S., Bailey, L., Cooker, L., Fox, S. & Bowman, A. (2015), 'Caring' across the International Baccalaureate Continuum. Available at: https://www.ibo.org/contentassets/952a2e6109b144ac86485780bfc8fbec/caring-across-the-continuum-eng.pdf (accessed 17 October 2020).

Stevenson, H., Shah, S., Bailey, L., Cooker, L., Winchip, E., & Karak, M. (2017), The International Baccalaureate Middle Years Programme (MYP) in the United Arab Emirates. Available at: https://ibo.org/contentassets/a7bc64e18f3a4a5493d4213f648f8b18/myp_uae_finalreport_en.pdf (accessed 17 October 2020).

Stobie, T. (2016), The curriculum battleground. In: M. Hayden & J. Thompson (eds), *International Schools: Current Issues and Future Prospects*, 53–70. London: Symposium Books Ltd.

Stolton, S. (2019), Call me Boris. *The Brussels Times*, 1 November. Available at: https://www.brusselstimes.com/brussels-behind-the-scenes/76819/call-me-boris/ (accessed 2 March 2020).

Sunder, S. (2013), The teacher's managed heart in an international school setting. *International Schools Journal*, 33(1), 82–6.

Tajfel, H. (1972), Some developments in European social psychology. *European Journal of Social Psychology*, 2(3), 307–21.

Tajfel, H. & Turner, J. C. (1979), An integrative theory of intergroup conflict. In: W. G. Austin & S. Worchel (ed), *The Social Psychology of Intergroup Relations*, 33–47. Monterey: Brooks-Cole.

Tanu, D. (2017), *Growing up in Transit: The Politics of Belonging at an International School*. New York: Berghahn Books.

Tarc, P. (2009), *Global Dreams, Enduring Tensions: International Baccalaureate in a Changing World*. New York: Peter Lang.

Tarc, P. & Mishra Tarc, A. (2015), Elite international schools in the Global South: Transnational space, class relationalities and the 'middling' international school teacher. *British Journal of Sociology of Education*, 36(1), 34–52.

Tarc, P., Mishra Tarc, A., & Wu, X. (2019), Anglo-Western international school teachers as global middle class: Portraits of three families. *Discourse: Studies in the Cultural Politics of Education*, 40(5), 666–81.

Tate, N. (2013), International education in a post-Enlightenment world. *Educational Review*, 65(3), 253–66.

The Telegraph (2016), The world's most exclusive boarding schools. *The Telegraph*, 15 August. Available at: https://www.telegraph.co.uk/education/2016/03/11/the-worlds-most-exclusive-boarding-schools/collge-du-lman-switzerland/ (accessed 11 February 2020).

Tikly, L. (2001), Globalisation and education in the postcolonial world: Towards a conceptual framework. *Comparative Education*, 37(2), 151–71.

Turner, C. (2019), China is growing fed up with British private schools 'creaming off' the best pupils, headteachers warned. *The Telegraph*, 1 October. Available at: https://www.telegraph.co.uk/news/2019/10/01/china-growing-fed-british-private-schools-creaming-best-pupils/ (accessed 5 February 2020).

Useem, R. H. & Downie R. D. (1976), Third-Culture Kids. *Today's Education*, 65(3), 103–5.

UWC (2021), *UWC History and Founding Ideas*. Available at: https://www.uwc.org/history (accessed 1 March 2021).

Velarde, J. (2017), Instructional leadership practices in international schools in Malaysia: A case study. *International Online Journal of Educational Leadership*, 1(1), 90–117.

Walker, A. & Quong, T. (1998), Valuing differences: Strategies for dealing with the tensions of educational leadership in a global society. *Peabody Journal of Education*, 73(2), 81–105.

Walker, G. (2016), International schools and international curricula. In: M. Hayden & J. Thompson (eds), *International Schools: Current Issues and Future Prospects*, 37–52. London: Symposium Books Ltd.

Ware, A. (2015), The great British education 'fraud' of the twentieth and Twenty-First Centuries. *The Political Quarterly*, 86(4), 475–84.

Waters, J. L. (2007), 'Roundabout routes and sanctuary schools': The role of situated educational practices and habitus in the creation of transnational professionals. *Global Networks*, 7(4), 477–97.

Waterson, M. (2016), The corporatisation of international schooling. In: M. Hayden & J. Thompson (eds), *International Schools: Current Issues and Future Prospects*, 185–214. Oxford: Symposium Books.

Weenink, D. (2008), Cosmopolitanism as a form of capital: Parents preparing their children for a globalizing world. *Sociology*, 42(6), 1089–106.

Wettewa, V. (2016), Postcolonial emotionalism in shaping education: An analysis of international school choice in Sri Lanka. *International Education Journal: Comparative Perspectives*, 15(1), 66–83.

Wettewa, V. & Bagnall, N. (2017), International school choice in Sri Lanka. *Current Politics and Economics of South, Southeastern, and Central Asia*, 26(4), 385–410.

Wickins, E. & Edwards, A. (2018), And a Green Tea Frappuccino: Developing the local dimension of international schools. In: K. J. Kennedy & J.C.-K. Lee (eds), *Routledge International Handbook of Schools and Schooling in Asia*, 261–71. Abingdon: Routledge.

Wiliam, D. (2013), *Principled Curriculum Design*. London: SSAT (The Schools Network) Limited.

Wright, E. & Lee, M. (2019), Re/producing the global middle class: International Baccalaureate alumni at 'world-class' universities in Hong Kong. *Discourse: Studies in the Cultural Politics of Education*, 40(5), 682–96.

Wright, K. & Buchanan, E. (2017), Education for international mindedness: Life history reflections on schooling and the shaping of a cosmopolitan outlook. *Current Issues in Comparative Education*, 20(1), 68–83.

Young, N. A. (2018), Departing from the beaten path: International schools in China as a response to discrimination and academic failure in the Chinese educational system. *Comparative Education*, 54(2), 159–80.

Zajda, J. (2020), Globalisation and neo-liberalism in higher education: Australia. In: J. Zajda (ed), *Globalisation, Ideology and Neo-Liberal Higher Education Reforms*, 47–57. Dordrecht: Springer.

Index

accidental teachers 67
Adams, M. 38
Adly Gamal, M. 84, 89
Ahmed, D. 29, 30, 144
Al Farra, S. 81
Allan, M. 80–1, 118, 138
American international school 58
Apple, M. W. 131, 147
Arabic language and culture 81, 84, 86, 106, 107
Auld, E. 135
Awang, S. 83
Ayling, P. 117–18

Bagnall, N. 115
Bahrain 86–7, 121
Ball, S. J. 29, 32
Barakat, M. 58
Bates, R. 27–8, 104, 116
Benham, M. 44
Benson, J. 43
Bernstein, B. 98, 108
Biesta, G. 139
Blackmore, J. 71
Bolay, M. 72, 103
Boltanski, L. 114
Bourdieu, P. 31, 33, 98, 114, 117, 131
Bowles, S. 33–4
Branksome Hall 17, 20, 45
Brooks, J. S. 58
Brown, C. 33, 35–7, 113
Brown, P. 138, 140
Buchanan, E. 101
Buheji, M. 29, 30, 144
Bunnell, T. 10, 17, 31, 49, 58, 62, 64, 67, 69, 71, 81, 95, 102
Burbules, N. C. 133
Burke, L. E. C. A. 82, 83, 87–8
Burns, E. 140
Burrows, M. 29

Caffyn, R. 45
Calnin, G. 57

Cambridge, J. 26, 135
Canterford, G. 119
Career related Programme (CP) 12
caring 37–8, 82, 118, 123, 126
Cheah, K. S. L. 83
China 19, 21–2, 36, 37, 53–4, 64, 66, 74, 85, 88, 89, 124, 134
Chua, Y. P. 83
civic multiculturalism 103–4
consumer culture 46
Cooker, L. 5, 37, 65–7, 74
corporate multiculturalism 103–4
correspondence theory 37–8
Cortazzi, M. 83
cosmopolitanism 31–3, 100, 102–3, 115, 116
Council of British International Schools (COBIS) 49
Council of International Schools 14
Courtois, A. 17
Covid-19 70, 110, 143, 144–7, 151–2
cultural
    capital 31–3
    diversity 58–9
    laundering 50
    linguistic and 85–6
    teaching and learning 83–5
    values and assumptions 81–2
curriculum 93–4, 111
    assessment and 109–11
    international and national 105–7
    for international-mindedness 99–105
    international schools 94–9

De Silva, M. 88–9
Deveney, B. 84, 118
Dickson, A. 120
Diploma Programme (DP) 12, 32, 83, 96, 103–5
diversity 13–15, 58–9
Doherty, C. 106–7
Donnelly, M. 17
Dubai 18

Dugonjić-Rodwin, L. 107
Dulwich College International 20–1
Dunne, S. 142
Durkheim, E. 138

Edwards, A. 87
Edwards, J. 142
Egypt 17, 58
Emenike, N. W. 82
Emirati school 54–6
English-language 33, 80, 142
Englishness 43, 50
English public schooling 21
ethnicity 116–19, 126–8
ethos 50–1
Europe 8, 18

Fanning, S. 140
Fertig, M. 44, 67, 95
Fieldwork Education 95, 98
Fimyar, O. 65
Fitzsimons, S. 80, 87
Fleer, M. 38
for-profit organizations 16–20, 43–7, 51–3, 59, 113
Foucault, M. 38, 131, 136
Frangie, M. 82

Gardner-McTaggart, A. 43, 50, 85–6, 98, 101
Garton, B. 119
gender difference 120
Gez, Y. N. 72
Gibson, M. 5, 43, 48, 49, 59, 122
Gilbertson, A. 134
Gillborn, D. 117
Gintis, H. 33–4
Global Competence 94
globalization 7, 25–8, 63, 75–6, 106, 114, 132–5, 137, 140, 141, 146–8, 150
Global Middle Class (GMC) 25, 28–33, 36, 37, 62, 70, 71, 98, 102, 104, 114, 116, 139, 149, 151, 152
Global Nomad 78
glocalization 27, 87
Gong, Y. 66
Goodhart, D. 75
governance 45–7
GREAT Britain Campaign 28
Green, B. 105–6

Growth Paradox 49
Gunesch, K. 100, 102

Hahn, K. 8, 14
Hallinger, P. 44–5, 51, 84
Hammad, W. 50
Hardman, O. T. J. 62–3
Hayden, M. 9, 14, 15, 18, 32, 67, 100, 148
Hayden, M. J. 100
higher education (HE) 136
Hill, I. 99
Hoechner, H. 27
host-country nationals 30, 36, 63, 73, 78, 79, 83, 89–90, 97, 113, 115, 118, 141, 144, 149, 152
Hughes, C. 79
hyperglobalist approach 132

identity 38
   teachers 64–8
iGCSEs 35, 93, 95–6, 110
imperial gaze 50
India 134
Indonesia 126–8
inequality 113–14, 120–1
   ethnicity 116–19
   social class 114–16
international A levels 95–6, 110
International Baccalaureate (IB) 4, 8, 11–13, 32, 35, 42, 43, 94–5, 100, 109, 143
   Learner Profile 34, 37, 94, 101, 143
   teachers 67
   and UAE 107–8
international education 135–8
internationalism 3, 10, 26, 42, 43, 68, 81, 89–91, 100, 113, 131, 133, 137, 138
international-mindedness 7, 8, 12, 32, 38, 43, 44, 67, 94, 98–105, 111, 123, 135, 145, 149
International Primary Curriculum (IPC) 13, 95
International School of Geneva 8, 11–12, 18, 94
international schools 7–11, 147–53
   and Covid-19 144–7, 151–2
   curriculum in 94–9
   diversity 13–15
   globalization and 132–4
   identity in 38

international and national curriculum 105–7
market for 15–19
social relations of 33–7
Islamic study 56–7, 84, 87, 89, 107

James, C. 18–19, 44, 47, 67, 95
Jing, Q. 99, 100, 102
Jin, L. 83
Jones, P. W. 137
Joslin, P. 67

Keeling, A. 15
Keller, D. 48
Khan, S. Z. 109
Kim, H. 46, 47, 115
Kong, L. 88–9
Koo, H. 28–30
Kuala Lumpur 123

Lai, C. 66
language and power 141–2
Lauder, H. 33, 35–7, 113
leadership
  and hierarchy 56–8
  style 51
Learner Profile 34, 37, 94, 101, 143
Ledger, S. 101, 103, 120
Lee, M. 32, 44–5, 51, 84
LGBTQ students 124–5
Lingard, B. 136
linguistic difference 119, 142
Li, Z. 66
Lowe, J. 35

MacDonald, J. 44
Machin, D. 47
Malaysia 14, 16, 20, 41, 51–3, 65, 73, 77, 83, 87, 89–90, 95, 119, 120, 122, 125–6, 150
Mansilla, V. B. 101
Marshall, H. 103
mass education systems 138
metro-rural disparities 120
micropolitics 41–5
  cultural diversity 58–9
  ethos 50–1
  governance 45–7
  leadership and hierarchy 56–8

school composition 48–50
Middle Years Programme (MYP) 12, 85, 107, 108
Mishra Tarc, A. 71–2, 128
mobility capital 70
Mobrand, E. 115
Mohamed, M. 136
Moret, J. 70
Morris, P. 135, 136
Morrow, R. A. 114
multiculturalism 103–4
Murakami-Ramalho, E. 44

National Curriculum 34, 95
neo-liberalism 26, 36, 38, 46, 61, 69, 79–80, 106, 114–15, 134, 138, 146–8
Newman, A. 27
Nigeria 82, 117
Nikita, D. P. 29, 32
Nord Anglia Education 19–20
not-for-profit organizations 13, 18, 47, 53–4, 109

O'Donoghue, T. 120
Olivier, J. 27
Olssen, M. 26

Pearson, R. F. 124
Perry, L. B. 120
Pinar, W. 106
Plowright, D. 82
Poole, A. 31, 38, 63, 64, 67–71, 116
postcolonial theory 88
post-Fordism 34
precariat 68–72
precarious privilege 72
Primary Years Programme (PYP) 12, 96, 108–9
Principals Training Center 42
Programme for International Student Assessment (PISA) 5, 28, 94, 102, 109, 136
pro-social learning 37–8

Qatar 82, 84, 89

resilience capital 71, 116
Resnik, J. 10, 13, 34–5, 37, 64, 103–4, 106, 124

Rey, J. 72, 103
Rockstuhl, T. 56
Russia 108–9

Sancho, D. 27
Sanderson, R. E. 43, 120
Savva, M. 64, 102
sceptical approach 132
school. *See also* international schools
   composition 48–50
   curriculum 94–9
   ethos 50–1
Sears, C. 142
Sellar, S. 136
Shah, S. 50
Shell Company 8
Sheppard, P. 18–19, 47
shura 56–7
Sidhu, R. K. 136–7
Singh. M. 99, 100, 102
Slough-Kuss, Y. 42–3
social class 114–16
social relations 33–7
Song, J. J. 115–16
South Korea 29, 30, 115–16
Standing, G. 68–9
Stanfield, D. 102
state regulatory powers 46
Steffens, N. K. 57
Steiner-Khamsi, G. 107
Stobie, T. 97–8
Sunder, S. 64

Tanu, D. 118
Tarc, P. 70, 71–2, 128, 143
Tate, N. 143
Taylors Group, The 20
teachers 61–3, 73–5
   identity 64–8
   precariat 68–72
   working 63–4
Thailand 84, 85, 118
Third Culture Kids (TCKs) 36, 54, 66, 78, 82, 140–1
Third Culture Teachers 66–7, 75
Thoenig, M. 27

Thompson, J. 9, 14, 15, 18, 26, 67, 135, 148
Tikly, L. 132
Torres, C. A. 114, 133
Trans-National Corporations (TNCs) 17
transnational education corporations 46
Type A school 14, 67, 68
Type B school 14, 67, 68
Type C school 14–15, 64, 67, 68, 70, 137

United Arab Emirates (UAE) 54–6, 107–8
United World College (UWC) 8, 11–12
US Department of Defence 8
US Department of Education 10

Verdier, T. 27
Vidovich, L. 120

Walker, A. 44–5, 84
Walker, G. 94–5
Ware, A. 30
Waters, J. L. 88
Waterson, M. 16–17, 46–7
Waves of education
   first 138
   fourth 139, 151
   second 138
   third 138–40
Weenink, D. 102–3
Westernization 77–81, 90–1
   cultural values and assumptions 81–2
   Malaysia and 89–90
   resisting 87–9
   teaching and learning 83–5
Wettewa, V. 115, 118
Whitehead, S. 43, 120
whiteness 117–18
Wickins, E. 87
Wiliam, D. 96
Wilson, D. 101
Woods, O. 88–9
Wright, E. 32
Wright, K. 101
Wu, X. 71–2

Yokohama International School 8
Young, N. A. 123–4

www.ingramcontent.com/pod-product-compliance
Lightning Source LLC
Chambersburg PA
CBHW061836300426
44115CB00013B/2413